FREEDOM
in CHRIST

PARTICIPANT'S GUIDE

**A 10-Week Life-Changing
Discipleship Course**

NEIL T. ANDERSON
& STEVE GOSS

BETHANYHOUSE
a division of Baker Publishing Group
Minneapolis, Minnesota

Published by Bethany House Publishers
11400 Hampshire Avenue South
Bloomington, Minnesota 55438
www.bethanyhouse.com

Bethany House Publishers is a division of
Baker Publishing Group, Grand Rapids, Michigan

Printed in the United States of America

ISBN 978-0-7642-1953-5

Cover design by Rob Williams, InsideOutCreativeArts

21 22 23 24 25   10 9 8 7 6

Contents

Comments From Participants

"I have a clear head, praise Jesus — it's
not been really clear for years!"

"Knowing who I am in Christ and accepting the truth of God
while rejecting the lies of the devil has changed my life."

"It is helping me to grow and mature as
a Christian as never before."

"My life has been transformed. It truly was like
walking from darkness back into light again."

"I was separated from the truth of God's love and
Jesus' liberation by a large wall of pain, wounds,
and lies. But the wall came tumbling down."

"It proved to be a pivotal point in my Christian life. . . .
I now feel that I have the abundant life which Christ
spoke of and which I have been yearning for."

Why Take Part In This Course?

The *Freedom In Christ Course* is for every Christian, from those who have been Christians for a long time to those who have only just made that decision, from those who are progressing steadily to those who feel stuck.

It is designed to help you:

- **break through to a greater level of spiritual maturity**
- **uncover any areas of deception holding you back**
- **resolve personal and spiritual conflicts**
- **learn strategies to renew your mind and break free from negative thinking and unhelpful patterns of behavior**

The course does not focus on how to behave but on how to believe. After all, Christ has already set us free (Galatians 5:1) and given us everything we need (2 Peter 1:3). It's just that sometimes it doesn't feel like it!

Many sense that they have not reached their full potential for God. Perhaps they feel "stuck" in habitual sin, negative thoughts, fears, unforgiveness, or condemnation. Yet they really want to grow and mature. This course will help you grasp the amazing truth of your new identity in Christ, teach you to uncover and resist the enemy's deception, and help you move on. It's not a "quick fix." But it is likely to revolutionize your Christian life.

How Can I Get The Most Out Of It?

Do your best to get to each session.

Read the accompanying books (see page 6) or **Victory Over The Darkness** and **The Bondage Breaker** by Neil Anderson to reinforce the teaching.

Get the accompanying app (see page 7) which has some fantastic tools to help you and will send you appropriate daily nuggets of truth while you are going through the course.

Be sure to go through *The Steps To Freedom In Christ*, a kind and gentle process during which you ask the Holy Spirit to show you any areas of your life where you may need to repent. Most groups schedule this between Sessions 7 and 8, and for many it is a life-changing experience.

The course includes strategies for standing firm in the freedom won and renewing your mind on an ongoing basis — make them part of your daily life.

Get More Out Of The Course

Steve Goss has written four slim, easy-to-digest books specifically for participants on the *Freedom In Christ Course*. They present the same teaching but in a different way with additional material so that you can take the message deeper. They are published by Monarch and are available from Freedom In Christ Ministries (see FICMinternational.org for details) and other booksellers.

Free to be Yourself — Enjoy your true nature in Christ
Many Christians act as they think a Christian should act — and find that they simply can't keep it up. They either drop out or burn out. True fruitfulness comes from realizing that we became someone completely new the moment we became Christians.
Corresponds to Part A (Sessions 1 to 2).

Win the Daily Battle — Resist and stand firm in God's strength
You are in a raging battle, whether you like it or not. Your only choice is to stand and fight or to become a casualty. Arrayed against you are the world, the devil, and the flesh but once you understand how they work and just who you are in Christ, you can expect to emerge victorious from every skirmish with them.
Corresponds to Part B (Sessions 3 to 5).

Break Free, Stay Free — Don't let the past hold you back
Every Christian has a past. It can hold us back big-time. Those of us with a lot of "stuff" know that only too well. But even those who have had a relatively trouble-free existence need to know how to resolve negative influences that stop us from moving on.
Corresponds to Part C (Sessions 6 to 8).

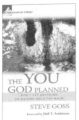

The You God Planned — Don't let anything hold you back
Once we have claimed our freedom in Christ, how do we remain in it and make fruitfulness a way of life? How do we know what God is calling us to be anyway? Are the goals we have for our lives in line with His goals? How can we stop others getting in the way? And how do we avoid getting in their way?
Corresponds to Part D (sessions 9 to 10).

The Freedom In Christ App

This specially-written app will become your indispensable companion as you progress through the *Freedom In Christ Course*:

- Get a daily nugget of truth tailored to where you are on the course delivered to your device
- Access the three key lists of Biblical truths
- Extra teaching films on key topics
- Powerful Stronghold-Buster Builder tool: find your Bible verses, create your stronghold-buster, and specify when you wish to be reminded to use it
- Sample songs from *Worship In Spirit And Truth*, the album written to accompany the course, and see films of the songwriters, Wayne and Esther Tester and Nicole C. Mullen, sharing why Freedom In Christ is so important to them personally (see pages 205–223)
- Get a daily devotional from Neil Anderson delivered to your device.

The app is free to download and use. There is a small charge to unlock some of the content. Search for "Freedom In Christ" in your app store. In case of difficulty, go to **FICMinternational. org/app** where you will find the app store links.

Meet The Presenters Of The Video

Steve Goss has a background in business and started Freedom In Christ's UK office in 1999, thinking that he could do it on Friday afternoons only. He is "still somewhat surprised" to find himself in full-time Christian ministry. Neil Anderson, Founder of Freedom In Christ Ministries, handed the international leadership of the ministry to Steve in 2012 and it now operates in around 40 countries. He and Zoë have been married for over 30 years and have two grown-up daughters and a pug. They are based in Berkshire, west of London, but travel extensively to minister on all five continents.

In the late '80s and early '90s you would have found **Daryl Fitzgerald** in a Christian hip-hop group called Transformation Crusade — he insists their music was better than their name! He and his wife Stephanie live in Nashville, Tennessee, USA, and have a passion for helping families and marriages. Daryl was a Family Pastor until 2016 when he and Stephanie joined the field staff of Freedom In Christ Ministries. They are the proud parents of five children, the three youngest of whom are in a pop, soul, and rock-n-roll band called The New Respects (which, some might say, is really quite a good name.)

Nancy Maldonado was born in the Andes mountains of Ecuador where she built forts and caught tadpoles with Rob, her childhood friend. Years later, the Swiss Alps would witness their engagement. They lived many adventures as missionaries in Spain, but they say their greatest adventure has been parenting Josue and Sofia in a postmodern secular society. Nancy is part of Freedom In Christ's international team and is specifically responsible for translating FIC materials into Spanish. She loves trying new recipes, discipling women, bright colors, and Earl Grey tea with milk.

See the presenters introduce themselves in a film on the FIC app.

Why Believe The Bible?

WHAT'S IT ABOUT?

This session is an optional introduction to the *Freedom In Christ Course*.

OBJECTIVE: To understand why it is perfectly reasonable to believe that the Bible is God's message to the people He created.

FOCUS VERSE: For the word of God is living and active. Sharper than any double-edged sword, it penetrates even to dividing soul and spirit, joints and marrow; it judges the thoughts and attitudes of the heart. (Hebrews 4:12)

FOCUS TRUTH: When it comes to books, the Bible is in a league of its own and there are several very good reasons for believing that it is God's message to the people He created.

 WELCOME

What is the best book you have ever read (apart from the Bible)?

 WORSHIP

Putting God right at the center of the course and opening our hearts to Him. Jeremiah 29:11–13, Psalm 33:4–7, Hebrews 4:12, Philippians 1:6.

WORD

Why Should We Trust The Bible?
The Bible is easily the most influential book ever written:

- it was the first book ever printed
- it has been translated into over 2,500 languages
- it contains over 750,000 words
- it would take you about 70 hours to read the whole Bible out loud

Even though it was written by 40 different people (from kings to fishermen) who lived over a period of 1,500 years on three continents, the great claim of the Bible is that, taken together as a whole, it is the message of God Himself to the people He created. To quote the Bible itself, "All Scripture is breathed out by God." (2 Timothy 3:16).

But why should we trust it?

PAUSE FOR THOUGHT 1

When was the first time that you heard about the Bible, read the Bible, or had it read to you?

Is there a Bible passage or verse that is particularly special to you? If so, read it to the group and explain briefly why it is so meaningful.

Why do you believe — or why do you currently struggle with the concept — that the Bible is "the inspired word of God"?

1. History Confirms The Bible
To date, the findings of archaeology have done nothing except verify the Bible's historical accuracy.

People doubted the existence of Sodom and Gomorrah, two cities mentioned in one of the oldest parts of the Bible, but in the mid-1970s a team of Italian archaeologists came across a library of 15,000 clay tablets dating back to around 2,500 BC which mentioned them.

The Old Testament mentions a people called "the Hittites" over 50 times but there was no evidence for their existence outside the Bible. Yet, during the 19th and 20th centuries, archaeologists found evidence that backed up the Bible's claims and even found the Hittites' capital city, Hittusa, in Northern Turkey.

In the Gospel of John (John 5:2–15), John gives a detailed description of a particular pool where Jesus performed a healing miracle, mentioning that it had five covered walkways supported by columns and that it was a place where invalids gathered hoping for a miracle because folklore said that occasionally the waters in the pool would be supernaturally stirred up and the first one into the water when that happened would get healed. For centuries, there was absolutely no evidence of this pool in Jerusalem. However, in the late 1800s, a pool with five covered walkways supported by columns was discovered 40 feet or so underground together with an inscription about the supposed healing properties of the waters.

Note: there are many information sources you can consult to confirm this and other examples mentioned. Your group leader will be able to recommend some.

Here's the main point: If the Bible is proved accurate in its historical detail, it's a strong reason for giving serious consideration to the things it reports that may seem out of the ordinary or impossible. And if the authors of the Bible are proved to be accurate in their historical detail, how can we pick and choose and say they cannot be right when they report things that were out of the ordinary, such as a healing, just because we suppose that "it can't have happened"?

2. What The Bible Said Would Happen Did Happen

The Bible is full of predictions about the future (prophecies) that came true, many of which seemed extremely unlikely to happen.

For example, in 586 BC, Ezekiel predicted the destruction of an ancient city called Tyre. He told them that God was saying this: "I will bring many nations against you, like the sea casting up its waves. They will destroy the walls of Tyre and pull down her towers; I will scrape away her rubble and make her a bare rock." (Ezekiel 26:3–4). Shortly afterward Nebuchadnezzar began a siege that lasted 13 years. The city fell as predicted, the inhabitants fled to a fortified island off the coast, and set up a new city. Ezekiel added (in verse 12) that the invaders would "throw your stones, timber and rubble into the sea." Two-hundred fifty years later, Alexander the Great attacked the island fortress. In order to do so, he had to build a causeway which involved scraping the old city back to a bare rock — a specific prediction — and throwing it all into the sea.

Many details of the life and death of Jesus Christ were written down accurately hundreds of years before His birth.

PAUSE FOR THOUGHT 2

Look up some of the following Old Testament prophecies:
Micah 5:2; Isaiah 7:14; Jeremiah 31:15; Psalm 41:9; Zechariah 11:12–13; Psalm 22:16-18 and Zechariah 12:10; Exodus 12:46 and Psalm 34:20; Psalm 22:18. From your knowledge of the story of Jesus, how were these prophecies fulfilled?

"History confirms the Bible and things predicted in it later happened." How do these two things help you believe the Bible really is God's message to us?

What are some of the reasons that people dismiss the claims of the Bible?

3. The Bible's Claim That Jesus Rose From The Dead Is Credible

The defining claim of the New Testament is that Jesus Christ rose from the dead. This is a startling claim, and many may simply dismiss it as impossible without even looking at the facts. But those with a genuinely open mind will surely want to look at the evidence.

The medical evidence seems to indicate that Jesus was, in fact, dead before He was put in the tomb — professional Roman soldiers with plenty of execution experience gave this verdict. It seems equally clear from the evidence that three days later the tomb was indeed empty. Even the authorities admitted it and said that the disciples must have stolen Jesus' body.

Jesus appeared to His disciples a few days after being subjected to the most brutal execution method known at that time. And He seemed absolutely fine, not like someone who'd nearly escaped death. In fact He appeared to over 500 people at the same time.

Peter, one of Jesus' disciples, wrote: "We did not follow cleverly invented stories when we told you about the power and coming of our Lord Jesus Christ, but we were eye-witnesses of his majesty" (2 Peter 1:16). Many of those eye-witnesses — including Peter — went on to die for their belief that Jesus rose from the dead. You don't go to your death for something that you're not absolutely certain about.

4. The Church Has Never Stopped Growing

If the Bible is God's Word, then you would expect the Church to be growing. Is that happening?

The Lausanne Statistical Task Force concluded that:

- The worldwide church took until 1900 to reach 2.5% of the world population;
- Then, in just 70 years it doubled to reach 5% of the world population;
- In the next 30 years — between 1970 and 2000 — it more than doubled again to reach 11.2% of the world population.

About a million people a week are becoming Christians. In fact, there are probably more Christians alive right now than have ever lived and died throughout the whole of history. The decline in the Church in the West is a historical anomaly that is far outweighed by the growth elsewhere.

The Church is the most dynamic organization the world has ever seen. It's never stopped growing and is growing faster today than ever before.

Jesus predicted all this in the Bible. He said, "I will build my church, and the gates of Hades will not overcome it" (Matthew 16:18).

5. The Truths In The Bible Change Lives Today

If the Bible is true, you'd expect to see an impact in people's daily lives too.

Those of us who believe that the Bible consists of a message from God Himself are not taking some blind "leap of faith." There is a perfectly logical and reasonable basis for what we believe. We've only had time to skim the surface, but there are plenty of resources available if you want to find out more.

The Rest Of The Course

If the Bible is true, then we'll find the principles it gives us for living truly life-changing. In the rest of the course we'll consider those principles.

The focus won't be on obeying rules or on our behavior but on what we **believe**. Jesus said, it is when we know the truth, that we will be truly free (John 8:32). When we get our beliefs right, our behavior will follow.

We will learn how becoming a Christian is the defining moment in our lives, how we became brand new people from the inside out, and why that means we can come to God any time we like without fear.

We'll find out how we can resolve the effects of even the deepest issues from the past and how we can deal with repeating patterns of getting stuck in stuff we'd rather not be in.

We'll also get to understand what God's purpose is for our lives. It may not be what you think!

REFLECTION

Spend some time thanking God for the Bible.

Then ask Him to continue to develop in you a thirst and longing to read and understand His Word in your day-to-day life.

WITNESS

If someone told you that they thought the Bible was "just a collection of myths and legends" what would you say to them?

 IN THE COMING WEEK

If you have never got to grips with reading the Bible regularly before, why not try reading a little bit each day? You could start with one of the Gospels: Matthew, Mark, Luke, or John. As you read, remind yourself of the truths we have looked at and that the Creator of the universe wants to speak to **you** through His Word, the Bible, **today**. Wow!

KEY TRUTHS

Jesus said that we will know the truth
and the truth will set us free!

In the first two sessions we look at some of the key truths
we need to know about what it means to be a Christian.

FREEDOM
IN CHRIST

Who Am I?

WHAT'S IT ABOUT?

OBJECTIVE: To realize that deep down inside we are now completely new creations in Christ, "holy ones" who are accepted, secure, and significant.

FOCUS VERSE: Therefore, if anyone is in Christ, he is a new creation. The old has passed away; behold, the new has come. (2 Corinthians 5:17 ESV)

FOCUS TRUTH: Your decision to follow Christ was the defining moment of your life and led to a complete change in who you now are.

It's time to start the Freedom In Christ app (see page 7)! Enter the date of today's session and for seven days it will give you some short nuggets of truth to consider.

Steve Goss has written four short books that correspond to the four parts of the course (see page 6). The first in the series, *Free To Be Yourself*, corresponds to Part A of the course (the first two sessions). Read up to page 59 in the book for the material that relates to this session.

WELCOME

Spend a couple of minutes in pairs finding out as much as you can about each other. Then, in no more than 30 seconds, answer this question about your partner. "Who is he/she?"

WORSHIP

God's plans and promises. Psalm 33:10–11, Job 42:2, Proverbs 19:21.

WORD

Who Are You Really?

Perhaps the most fundamental truth we need to know is who we are. What makes up the real "me" or "you"?

The Original Design

We were made "in God's image" (Genesis 1:26), and God is spirit. So at the most fundamental level of our being we too have a **spiritual** nature. It is not our body, our outer person, that is created in the image of God; it's our inner person.

Scientists confirm that our mitochondrial DNA proves that we are all descended from the same woman and our Y-chromosomes prove that we are all descended from the same man. The Bible tells us that our ultimate ancestors were called Adam and Eve. Christians disagree about exactly how God created them but we all agree that God inspired their story to be written down to communicate some very significant truth.

Adam's spirit — his inner person, the core of his being — was connected to his body. In other words he was **physically** alive. Just as we are. But Adam's spirit was also connected to God. Which meant that he was also **spiritually** alive. That is how we were designed to be too: on the one hand our spirit is connected to our physical body, and on the other hand our spirit is connected to God.

This spiritual connection to God gave Adam three very significant things:

1. Acceptance

He had an intimate relationship with God. He could talk with Him at any time and have His full attention.

2. Significance

He was given a purpose: to rule over the birds of the sky, the beasts of the field and the fish of the sea (Genesis 1:26).

3. Security

He was totally safe and secure in God's presence. Everything he needed was provided for — food, shelter, companionship — everything!

You were created for that kind of life: complete acceptance by God and other people; significance — a real purpose; and absolute security — no need to worry about a single thing.

The Consequence Of The Fall

Adam and Eve were told, "You must not eat from the tree of the knowledge of good and evil, for when you eat of it you will surely die" (Genesis 2:17).

They died spiritually. The connection that their spirit had to God was broken and they were separated from God. Consequently, all their descendants were born physically alive but spiritually dead.

The **acceptance** they enjoyed, that amazing intimate moment-by-moment relationship with God, changed into a crushing sense of rejection and we all know that feeling.

That sense of **significance** was replaced by a sense of guilt and shame and we're all born with it.

And that sense of **security** turned to fear. The first emotion expressed by Adam was, "I was afraid" (Genesis 3:10). "Don't be afraid" is the most repeated commandment in the Bible.

So all of us are born into an environment that's not at all like the one we were designed for. Instinctively we want to find our way back to the acceptance, significance, and security we were meant to have.

PAUSE FOR THOUGHT 1

What prompted you to come to the *Freedom In Christ Course* and what are your hopes for it?

What were the consequences of Adam and Eve's sin? What are the ways it caused their relationship with God to change?

What sort of things in our daily lives promise to make us feel accepted, significant, and secure?

What Jesus Came To Do

The only solution to the predicament that we've looked at is to restore our relationship with God, to become spiritually alive again.

That's why God sent Jesus. Like Adam at the very beginning He was both physically and spiritually alive. But unlike Adam, Jesus never sinned.

Why did Jesus come? To forgive my sins? Well, yes, but that was just a means to an end. Jesus Himself said, "I have come that they may have life, and have it to the full" (John 10:10).

What did Adam lose? **Life**. What did Jesus come to give us? **Life**.

When we become Christians our spirit is reconnected to God's Spirit. At that moment we get back the life we were always meant to have with its acceptance, significance, and security. Eternal life is not just something you get when you die. It's a whole different quality of life **right now**.

A Saint — Not A Sinner

So, who are you? The moment you became a Christian was the defining moment of your life. Everything changed for you. The language the Bible uses is dramatic:

> If anyone is in Christ, he is a new creation; the old has gone, the new has come! (2 Corinthians 5:17)

Can you be partly old creation and partly new? No!

> For you were once darkness, but now you are light in the Lord. (Ephesians 5:8)

Can you be both light and darkness? Not according to that verse.

Many of us have come to think of ourselves as "a sinner saved by grace." You certainly **were** a sinner, and you were saved by grace alone. But, here's an interesting verse:

> While we were still sinners, Christ died for us. (Romans 5:8)

It seems to imply that we're no longer sinners. In the New Testament, the word "sinner" appears over 300 times and is clearly a shorthand way of referring to people who are not yet Christians. You never see it applied to a Christian, at least not in terms of who they are **now**, only in terms of who they used to be.

There's another word that is shorthand for believers and you'll find it over 200 times. Traditionally in English this word has been translated "saint." It means "holy one."

Yes, you are holy. Set apart for God. Special. At the moment you became a Christian — even if you can't pinpoint the exact moment — you became completely new in your inner person. Who you are deep down inside changed from being someone who couldn't help but displease God to someone who is accepted, significant, and secure in Christ.

Galatians 3:27 says that we have "clothed ourselves with" Christ. Perhaps you have understood that to mean that you're still the same dirty, rotten no-good person deep down inside, but it's all covered up by Christ, so that when God looks at you, He doesn't really see you, He sees Jesus. But that's not at all what the Bible says. It's more like the story Jesus told about a son who messed up badly and came crawling back home dirty, smelly, and broken, expecting to be punished. His father unexpectedly welcomed him with open arms and within a few minutes of his arrival gave him a fine, expensive robe to wear (Luke 15:22).

Did the robe make him acceptable because it covered up all the dirt? No. The dirt was on the outside. It wasn't the robe that made him a son. He was given the robe because he was a son. It was the appropriate dress for a son.

Regardless of the mess you may have made or how bad you feel about yourself, the truth is that, if you have accepted Jesus as your Lord, you are now a son or daughter of God Himself. You're righteous, clean, and holy on the inside. You can clothe yourself with Christ because at the deepest level of your being He has already made you holy. When God the Father looks at you now, He doesn't see Christ covering your mess. He sees you just as you are: a new creation, holy, wonderful. And He delights in you.

Who you are now is a **fact** and Satan can't change it. But if he can get you to believe a lie about who you are, he can cripple your walk with God.

No child of God is inferior or useless, but if Satan can get you to believe that you are, that's how you'll act.

No child of God is dirty or abandoned any more. But if Satan can get you to believe that you are, that's how you'll act.

"You don't know what's been done to me." It doesn't change who you are in Christ. "You don't know what failures I've had as a Christian." It doesn't change who you are in Christ.

Jesus loved you when you were still a sinner. He's not going to stop now that you're a saint.

"But what about my future sins?" When Jesus died once for all, how many of your sins were future? All of them!

You're not saved by how you **behave** but by what you **believe**. And life as a Christian is more of the same. It's not about trying to behave differently. It's about knowing the truth, which then works out into your behavior. This course is not about learning to behave differently but to believe differently.

PAUSE FOR THOUGHT 2

John 10:10 says that Jesus came to bring us life in all its fullness. What do you think that might look like in practice?

How might knowing that we are "saints" or "holy ones" instead of "sinners" change how we see ourselves?

What are some of the things that could prevent us from fully knowing that we are now new creations in Christ who are completely forgiven?

What Happens When I Go Wrong?

One of the main problems we have with seeing ourselves as saints rather than sinners is that we are painfully aware that we still sin. You may have a problem with snoring or burping, but that doesn't mean you have to introduce yourself to people by saying, "Hi, my name is X and I'm a snorer / burper!" You may snore or burp but that's not who you **are**. It's what you **do**. There is a big difference between the two.

It's what we are deep down in our inner person that defines our identity, not what we do. If you are a Christian, at the very core of your being you now share in God's divine nature. We are now new creations; the old has gone, the new has come.

However, that doesn't mean that we are living in a state of sinless perfection. The Bible is clear: "If we claim to be without sin, we deceive ourselves and the truth is not in us" (1 John 1:8). We will go wrong from time to time.

Perhaps an accurate way to describe us would be "saints who sometimes sin."

Sin is a serious matter. It gives the devil a foothold in our lives, stops us being fruitful, and disrupts the harmony of our fellowship with God. But it doesn't fundamentally change our relationship with Him.

When you were born again, you became God's child. Spiritually speaking you received His DNA — God's own Spirit lives in you (Romans 8:9) and you now share His very nature (2 Peter 1:4). Nothing can separate you from God's love (Romans 8:39). No one can snatch you out of His hand (John 10:28).

When we do wrong, we need simply to go to our loving Father, agree with Him that we were wrong, change our thinking about the sin, turn away from it, and know our sin is already forgiven because of Christ's death.

Nothing you do can make God love you any more — or any less. If you were the only person in the whole world who needed Christ to die, He would have died just for you. That's how special you are!

Are You "In Christ"?

Does all we have been looking at apply to you? If you are a Christian the answer is a definite yes — but if you are not a Christian it does not yet apply.

What is a Christian? Someone who chooses to believe that Jesus Christ is the Son of God and has made a definite decision to put Him in charge of their life. If you are not certain that you are a Christian or you know you are not, and you want to take that step, you can do it right now. It's not complicated. But it will transform you from the inside out. No one is too bad or has gone so far away from God that they are disqualified. It's open to absolutely everyone. No exceptions.

Simply speak to Jesus out loud or in your mind in normal everyday language. Tell Him that you receive the free gift of spiritual life that He came to give you, ask Him to forgive everything you have ever done wrong, and tell Him that you are making a choice to put Him in charge of your life.

You could, for example, use these words:
"Thank you, Jesus, Son of God, for dying in my place to take away all of my sin. Right now I accept Your gifts of life and forgiveness. I choose to make You Lord of my life so that I can become someone completely new. Thank You that I am now Your holy child and that I belong to You."

If you have sincerely taken that step (whether you did it today or 80 years ago), all of the statements we read in the "Who I Am In Christ" list now definitely apply to you!

REFLECTION

Get together with one other person and have the first person read the "Who I Am In Christ" statements to the other changing "I am" to "You are." Then swap around.

Spend a few minutes discussing the statements and the verses they are based on. Share which ones impacted you and why. Spend some time praying for each other, that you will have a deeper understanding that your significance, security, and acceptance are found in Him.

 WITNESS

If you were asked by a neighbor to explain the difference between a Christian and someone who is not yet a Christian, what would you say? Do you think that a Christian is in any way better than a non-Christian? What would you say to someone who asks you, "Why should I become a Christian?"

IN THE COMING WEEK

Read the "Who I Am In Christ" list out loud every day. Then pick one of the truths that is particularly meaningful to you and spend some time reading it in its context and asking God to help you understand it more fully.

Who I Am In Christ

I Am Accepted

I renounce the lie that I am rejected, unloved, or shameful. In Christ I am accepted.
God says:

I am God's child (John 1:12)

I am Christ's friend (John 15:5)

I have been justified (Romans 5:1)

I am united with the Lord and I am one spirit with Him (1 Corinthians 6:17)

I have been bought with a price: I belong to God (1 Corinthians 6:19–20)

I am a member of Christ's body (1 Corinthians 12:27)

I am a saint, a holy one (Ephesians 1:1)

I have been adopted as God's child (Ephesians 1:5)

I have direct access to God through the Holy Spirit (Ephesians 2:18)

I have been redeemed and forgiven of all my sins (Colossians 1:14)

I am complete in Christ (Colossians 2:10)

I Am Secure

I renounce the lie that I am guilty, unprotected, alone, or abandoned. In Christ I am secure.

God says:

I am free from condemnation (Romans 8:1–2)

I am assured that all things work together for good (Romans 8:28)

I am free from any condemning charges against me (Romans 8:31–34)

I cannot be separated from the love of God (Romans 8:35–39)

I have been established, anointed, and sealed by God (2 Corinthians 1:21–22)

I am confident that the good work God has begun in me will be perfected
(Philippians 1:6)

I am a citizen of heaven (Philippians 3:20)

I am hidden with Christ in God (Colossians 3:3)

I have not been given a spirit of fear, but of power, love, and self-control
(2 Timothy 1:7)

I can find grace and mercy to help in time of need (Hebrews 4:16)

I am born of God and the evil one cannot touch me (1 John 5:18)

I Am Significant

I renounce the lie that I am worthless, inadequate, helpless, or hopeless. In Christ I am significant.

God says:

I am the salt of the earth and the light of the world (Matthew 5:13–14)

I am a branch of the true vine, Jesus, a channel of His life (John 15:1, 5)

I have been chosen and appointed by God to bear fruit (John 15:16)

I am a personal, Spirit-empowered witness of Christ's (Acts 1:8)

I am a temple of God (1 Corinthians 3:16)

I am a minister of reconciliation for God (2 Corinthians 5:17–21)

I am a fellow worker with God (2 Corinthians 6:1)

I am seated with Christ in the heavenly realms (Ephesians 2:6)

I am God's workmanship, created for good works (Ephesians 2:10)

I may approach God with freedom and confidence (Ephesians 3:12)

I can do all things through Christ who strengthens me! (Philippians 4:13)

I am not the great "I Am," but by the grace of God I am what I am (Exodus 3:14; John 8:24, 28, 58; 1 Corinthians 15:10)

Choosing To Believe The Truth

WHAT'S IT ABOUT?

OBJECTIVE: To understand that everyone lives by faith in something or someone and that faith in God is no more than finding out what is already actually true and choosing to believe and act on it.

FOCUS VERSE: Without faith it is impossible to please God, because anyone who comes to him must believe that he exists and that he rewards those who earnestly seek him. (Hebrews 11:6)

FOCUS TRUTH: God is truth. Find out what He has said is true and choose to believe it, whether it feels true or not, and your Christian life will be transformed.

> If you are reading the FREEDOM IN CHRIST DISCIPLESHIP SERIES books, read pages 60–93 of *Free To Be Yourself* for the material that corresponds to this session.

 WELCOME

Have you had a prayer answered recently? Share the story briefly.

Do you believe that an atheist has more or less faith than a Christian? What about a Hindu or a Muslim? What about someone who "just doesn't know"?

 WORSHIP

Realizing just how much God loves us and delights in us. Ephesians 3:16–19, Zephaniah 3:17, 2 Corinthians 3:18, Hebrews 12:1–2, Psalm 103:8–17.

WORD

Faith Is A Critical Issue

As we saw in the last session, if you know Jesus, you are a holy one. Whether it feels like it or not!

It doesn't make any difference whether you perform great one day, and mess up the next. God will still love you because that's His nature. He is love.

However, God's love for you on its own doesn't mean that you will be the person He wants you to be and that you will do the things that He has prepared for you. That's all about the choices you make. And the choices you make come down to what you believe; what you really believe, not necessarily what you **think** or what you **say** you believe.

If you want to know what someone really believes, don't listen to what they say but look at what they actually **do**.

Faith Is Simply Believing What Is Already True

"Without faith it is impossible to please God" (Hebrews 11:6).

Faith is finding out what is already true and making a choice to believe it.

In 1 Samuel 17 the Israelites were in a battle with the Philistine army. The Philistines were saying, "We don't want a blood-bath. Just have your best soldier fight our best soldier one-on-one, and the winner takes all." They had a secret weapon, a giant called Goliath. They thought no one could fight against him and win. The Israelite army was completely afraid.

But then comes a young boy, David, who pulls out his sling and says, "How dare you challenge the armies of the living God?" and kills Goliath.

David and the Israelite army were threatened by the same situation. The Israelite army saw the giant in relationship to themselves and were in a panic. But David saw the giant in relationship to God and was at peace.

David saw the situation as it really was. Faith is simply recognizing what is already actually true. The message of this session is simple: find out from God what is already true; choose to believe it whether it feels true or not; and it will transform your Christian life.

Everyone Lives And Operates By Faith

The issue of faith is not that we believe. Everyone believes in something or someone.

Some people choose to believe that there's no such thing as a God, that we've evolved from animals. That's faith.

The Critical Issue Is Who Or What We Believe In

You might believe that you can fly a plane across the Atlantic Ocean by pedaling it. You might have more faith to believe that it will work than anyone who has ever lived. But actually it won't work.

The critical issue with faith is not so much **that** we believe but **what** we believe. It's who or what we believe in that determines whether our faith will actually work.

In 1 Kings 18 Elijah and the prophets of Baal decided to hold a competition to see whose God was real. They both set up altars and threw a dead bull on it to be sacrificed. They were both to ask their god to send fire from heaven to burn it up. There were about 450 prophets of Baal. They danced and danced and called out to Baal but nothing happened. Then they cut themselves with spears and called out louder. Nothing. It went on all day but they didn't get an answer. Then it was Elijah's turn. He called on God and immediately fire came from heaven and burned up not only the bull but the wood and the stones!

Who had more faith? Actually we don't know. The prophets of Baal clearly had great faith in Baal but it made no difference — because Baal wasn't real.

Jesus said that we only need faith the size of a mustard seed to move a mountain (Matthew 17:20). Elijah may only have had a little bit of faith but He was calling on the true and living God. It doesn't depend on how large our faith is but on who we put our faith in. It's not our power that moves the mountain — it's God's.

Hebrews 13:8: "Jesus Christ is the same yesterday and today and forever." That's why He is the one thing we can put our faith in who will never fail us. He has never failed to be and do all that He said He would be and do. And He never changes.

PAUSE FOR THOUGHT 1

"If you want to know what someone really believes, don't listen to what they say, but look at what they actually do." Spend some time discussing this thought.

God asks us to believe what the Bible says is true, even when it might not feel true. Share about a time when you chose to override your feelings and acted by faith instead.

"It takes more faith to believe that there is no God than to believe in God." What do you think about this statement?

How Faith Grows

"Oh, if only I could have faith like so-and-so." You can! Faith is just making a choice to believe what God says.

It's great to memorize Bible verses and take part in a Bible study. But your faith grows when you take that verse or that truth you learned and put it into practice — and you find that God does not let you down.

As you get to know that God, the object of your faith, really can be trusted with absolutely anything, you will trust Him for bigger and bigger things. But start where you are right now.

Have you ever wondered how Abraham could contemplate sacrificing his son Isaac? He had come to learn through experience that God was loving and could be trusted.

You start with what God has said is true and you choose to believe it. Don't start with what you feel — you'll be all over the place!

You don't feel your way into good behavior — you behave your way into good feelings. Your feelings will follow in due course.

What are some of the ways our faith grows?

In what circumstances or seasons in your life have you noticed your faith grow the most?

What are some of the ways you have discovered that help you get to know God better?

Faith Is Demonstrated By Actions

In the Bible, the words "faith," "trust," and "believe" are all the same word in the original Greek. That's important to know because in English when you say that you believe something, it doesn't carry the same connotation as to trust in something, does it? But faith is not simply agreeing with something intellectually. It's a reliance that you demonstrate by actions.

"Faith by itself, if it is not accompanied by action, is dead. But someone will say, 'You have faith: I have deeds.' Show me your faith without deeds, and I will show you my faith by what I do" (James 2:17–18).

No matter what we **say**, it's what we **do** that shows what we really believe. If you want to know what you really believe, look at what you do.

It's when we find ourselves in difficult times that it can potentially grow the most. Maybe a health scare, financial concerns, or an uncertain future perhaps.

It's in these times that we have to choose whether to put our faith in God or in something else.

So, you can see that the question of how much faith you have is in your hands. It all depends on choosing to believe the truth and putting it into practice.

On the Freedom In Christ app, you'll find a film, "Who Is Responsible For What?," containing some additional teaching from Steve on this.

Every Christian can become a mature, fruitful disciple. Everyone can resist temptation, get out of hopelessness, leave behind negative behavior and past influences, and move on. You don't need some special anointing from God. You just need to know what is already true, choose to believe it, and act on it.

There's nothing magical about reading out loud lists such as "Twenty 'Cans' Of Success." The truth in them will only have an effect on your life to the extent that you choose to believe it. But reading the lists out loud is a great way to affirm that you are making that choice.

Elijah said: "How long will you waver between two opinions? If the Lord is God follow Him; but if Baal is God, follow him" (1 Kings 18:21). Will you take this opportunity to make a new commitment to base your life completely on what God says is true, regardless of your feelings and regardless of the opinions of others?

REFLECTION

In your group read the Twenty "Cans" Of Success. Pause after each one to allow people to share why that truth is particularly meaningful to them.

Which truth is most significant to you? Write it down and personalize it, for example, "Why should I, Nancy, say I can't when the Bible says I can do all things through Christ who strengthens me? (Philippians 4:13)" Take time to digest and enjoy this truth, asking God to help you receive it in your spirit.

WITNESS

Think of someone you know who is not yet a Christian. What does the Bible say about why they don't yet believe (see 2 Corinthians 4:4, Romans 10:14–15)? Write a prayer you could pray that specifically asks God to do something about the things that are stopping them from believing. Then take God at His word and pray it!

IN THE COMING WEEK

Every day read the Twenty "Cans" Of Success list out loud. Then pick one of the truths that is particularly appropriate to you and make a decision to believe it regardless of feelings and circumstances. If you can find a way of stepping out in faith in some practical way based on that truth, so much the better!

Twenty "Cans" Of Success

1. Why should I say I can't when the Bible says I can do all things through Christ who gives me strength (Philippians 4:13)?

2. Why should I lack when I know that God shall supply all my needs according to His riches in glory in Christ Jesus (Philippians 4:19)?

3. Why should I fear when the Bible says God has not given me a spirit of fear, but one of power, love, and a sound mind (2 Timothy 1:7)?

4. Why should I lack faith to fulfill my calling knowing that God has allotted to me a measure of faith (Romans 12:3)?

5. Why should I be weak when the Bible says that the Lord is the strength of my life and that I will display strength and take action because I know God (Psalm 27:1; Daniel 11:32)?

6. Why should I allow Satan supremacy over my life when He that is in me is greater than he that is in the world (1 John 4:4)?

7. Why should I accept defeat when the Bible says that God always leads me in triumph (2 Corinthians 2:14)?

8. Why should I lack wisdom when Christ became wisdom to me from God and God gives wisdom to me generously when I ask Him for it (1 Corinthians 1:30; James 1:5)?

9. Why should I be depressed when I can recall to mind God's loving kindness, compassion, and faithfulness and have hope (Lamentations 3:21–23)?

10. Why should I worry and fret when I can cast all my anxiety on Christ who cares for me (1 Peter 5:7)?

11. Why should I ever be in bondage knowing that, where the Spirit of the Lord is, there is freedom (2 Corinthians 3:17; Galatians 5:1)?

12. Why should I feel condemned when the Bible says I am not condemned because I am in Christ (Romans 8:1)?

13. Why should I feel alone when Jesus said He is with me always and He will never leave me nor forsake me (Matthew 28:20; Hebrews 13:5)?

14. Why should I feel accursed or that I am the victim of bad luck when the Bible says that Christ redeemed me from the curse of the law that I might receive His Spirit (Galatians 3:13–14)?

15. Why should I be discontented when I, like Paul, can learn to be content in all my circumstances (Philippians 4:11)?

16. Why should I feel worthless when Christ became sin on my behalf that I might become the righteousness of God in Him (2 Corinthians 5:21)?

17. Why should I have a persecution complex knowing that nobody can be against me when God is for me (Romans 8:31)?

18. Why should I be confused when God is the author of peace and He gives me knowledge through His indwelling Spirit (1 Corinthians 14:33; 1 Corinthians 2:12)?

19. Why should I feel like a failure when I am a conqueror in all things through Christ (Romans 8:37)?

20. Why should I let the pressures of life bother me when I can take courage knowing that Jesus has overcome the world and its tribulations (John 16:33)?

THE WORLD, THE FLESH, AND THE DEVIL

Every day we struggle against three things that conspire to push us away from truth. Understanding how the world, the flesh, and the devil work will enable us to renew our minds and stand firm.

The World's View Of Truth

WHAT'S IT ABOUT?

OBJECTIVE: To understand that Christians need to make a definite decision to turn away from believing what the world teaches and choose instead to believe what God says is true.

FOCUS VERSE: Do not conform to the pattern of this world, but be transformed by the renewing of your mind. Then you will be able to test and approve what God's will is — his good, pleasing and perfect will. (Romans 12:2)

FOCUS TRUTH: The world we grew up in influenced us to look at life in a particular way and to see that way as "true." However, if it doesn't stack up with what God says is true, we need to reject it and bring our beliefs into line with what really is true.

> The book *Win The Daily Battle* contains more information on this section of the course. Read pages 11–42 for this session.

WELCOME

If you could go anywhere in the world, where would you choose?

Do you think that the way you look at the world and what you believe would be very different if you had been brought up in a different culture?

WORSHIP

The uniqueness of Jesus. John 14:6, Ephesians 1:17–23, 1 Corinthians 1:30, Philippians 2:5–11.

WORD

What Is "The World"?

The world is the system or culture we grew up in and live in. That will vary greatly according to where you are from and when you were born.

Satan is "the ruler of this world" (John 12:31) and works through it.

It uses three main tactics to try to divert us from the truth.

Tactic 1: Promising To Meet Our Deepest Needs

We were created to have the kind of life Adam had: 100% acceptance, the highest significance, perfect security. But that wasn't the life we were born into. From our first breath we didn't have the spiritual connection to God that we were meant to have. Yet we were created with those in-built needs for acceptance, significance, and security that our connection with God would have fulfilled.

When we were growing up and instinctively started looking to fulfill those deep needs for acceptance, significance, and security, up popped the world and said, "No problem! I'll show you how to get those."

It feeds us false formulas:

> **Performance + accomplishments = significance**
> **Status + recognition = security**
> **Appearance + admiration = acceptance**

Those are lies. But in the absence of a spiritual connection to God, we naturally fell for them. Or as Paul put it, we naturally "followed the ways of this world" (Ephesians 2:2).

The world has a kind of one-two punch. On the one hand it makes us feel insignificant, insecure, and that nobody likes us. Then it offers us ways that promise to fix it: dress in fashionable brands, hang out with the elite. But they don't work.

Do not love the world or anything in the world. If anyone loves the world, love for the Father is not in them. For everything in the world — the lust of the flesh, the lust of the eyes, and the pride of life — comes not from the Father but from the world. The world and its desires pass away, but whoever does the will of God lives forever. (1 John 2:15–17)

There are three channels through which the world works: the lust of the flesh, the lust of the eyes, and the pride of life. They are the same channels that Satan used when he tempted Eve and again when he appeared to Jesus in the wilderness and tempted Him.

The Lust Of The Flesh

We'll look at the flesh as an enemy in its own right in the next session. But let's notice for now that the lust of the flesh is linked to the world. The more we buy into the world's lies and act on them, the more unhelpful patterns of thinking become established in our minds, which then become default ways of behaving.

The Lust Of The Eyes

The world shows me things that it claims will meet those legitimate needs for acceptance, significance, and security that God created me to have. It tries to get our attention with bright, new, attractive things. Airbrushed models make us feel we have to look a certain way and create anxiety about aging. Ultimately they don't lead us into the bright future they promise but into darkness and confusion.

The Pride Of Life

This is the temptation to boast about our life, based on the lie that it is possessions, achievements, or connections that make us significant.

When we feel the need to boast about what we have, our achievements, or who we know, we show our insecurity. We don't need a crutch to bolster our self-image because we are now holy, pleasing to God, and completely secure in Him!

PAUSE FOR THOUGHT 1

In what ways has the world tried to make you feel insignificant, insecure, and unloved?

In what ways has the world promised you significance, security, and acceptance? Do you recognize these "false formulas"?

> Performance + accomplishments = significance
>
> Status + recognition = security
>
> Appearance + admiration = acceptance

How can you counteract "the lust of the flesh, the lust of the eyes, and the pride of life" (1 John 2:15–17)?

Tactic 2: Painting A Complete But False Picture Of Reality

Have you ever put on a virtual reality headset? Rather than simply watching a movie or a sporting event you can have the impression that you are right in it. One of the pioneers of virtual reality says that the goal is to make technology that's as real as real life with none of the limitations. But of course it won't be real. It will just **feel** real.

And that's essentially the second tactic of the world: to give you a distorted view of reality but feed it to you as the real thing. In effect it gives you a virtual reality headset but you don't know you're wearing it. This virtual reality headset is called your "worldview."

Just as we pick up things like language from our environment, we also pick up beliefs, values, and ways of behaving. We are influenced by our family, our schooling, our friends, the media.

Without even realizing it, we develop a way of looking at reality that we believe is true. But if your worldview is faulty, it will lead to faulty judgments about what happens in your life.

There are thousands of different worldviews but let's look at the most common to understand how they work.

1. A Non-Western Worldview

If you were brought up in Africa or Eastern cultures you may well have absorbed the belief that the universe is controlled by a kind of universal power that runs through everything and by spirits of many types.

If something bad happened to you — let's say you suddenly became ill — you would pass that bad experience through your virtual reality goggles to make sense of it and you would probably begin to suspect that someone might be manipulating this universal power or the spirits against you by cursing you or doing some kind of magic.

Just as you might turn to an electrician to sort out problems with the power in your house, you would probably turn to a sort of cosmic electrician — a shaman or witch doctor — to sort out the problems with this universal power.

If this is how you see reality, chances are that you will be living in constant fear that someone else might have a better control of the powers or that you might somehow unwittingly upset a spirit that would then turn against you.

2. The Western Worldview

Most people brought up in the West don't turn to a witch doctor if things start to go wrong. Instead we tend to look for logical reasons and try to fix the problem. That's because we have been fed a different view of reality by the world. It's a worldview that tells us that what is real can only be known through scientific methods. If we are ill we'll turn to a doctor who will use scientific methods to try to make us better.

In this worldview, it's still just about OK to believe in God and other supernatural things but we come to believe that they have no real bearing on our daily life. It's generally thought, for example, that we can leave spiritual questions out of our children's education without losing anything that really matters.

Someone said, "I believe in God. But I'm a practicing atheist" and that would be true of many.

3. The Postmodern Worldview

But culture is always changing and another worldview — usually called the "Postmodern" worldview — has been emerging in the West in recent decades which is something of a reaction against past generations' reliance on scientists and experts. After all what experts say has all too often turned out to be wrong.

Whereas previous generations saw truth as something revealed by God or discovered by science, increasingly we test whether an idea is valid or not purely on the basis of our own personal experience. If it feels good to me, it's OK.

Politicians can say what people want to hear even if it flies in the face of facts and get a strong following. Groups on social media promote even the most outlandish views and members reinforce each other's beliefs.

That is why Christians are under pressure to agree that all religions are equally true. Saying that we respect the right of other people to different beliefs and that we are happy to dialogue with them is no longer enough. There is a pressure to agree that their beliefs are just as "true" as our own.

Younger Christians are happy to say that Jesus is **their** truth but hesitate to go further and talk about Him as **the** truth.

This has led to what you might call "extreme tolerance" where practically any behavior is acceptable. In fact the only thing that is seen as wrong is saying that what someone else is doing is wrong!

The bottom line is that people are increasingly absorbing into their worldview a belief that there is no real, solid, undergirding truth.

The Biblical Worldview: Truth Does Exist

Which worldview is right? None of them!

If we were to take that virtual reality headset off, get rid of the values and beliefs that our own particular culture instilled in us, what would the world actually look like?

The Bible claims to be God's revelation of reality to the people He created. If that is right, then taking off that headset would mean that what we would see would correspond exactly to what the Bible tells us. That what the Bible says is "how it really is."

Jesus said, "I am the way and the truth and the life. No one comes to the Father except through me" (John 14:6). What! Are we saying that only one view of reality can be right? Isn't that a bit, well, intolerant?

Consider the most important question facing everybody in the world: What happens when you die?

- Hinduism teaches that when a soul dies it is reincarnated in another form.
- Christianity teaches that souls spend eternity in either heaven or hell.
- Spiritists think we float around as ghosts.
- Atheists believe that we have no soul and that when we die our existence simply ends.

Can all those things be true at the same time? To put it another way, does what you believe will happen to you when you die make any difference to what will actually happen? Or will the same thing happen to everyone when they die regardless of what they believed before the event?

Surely, if Hindus are right, we will all be reincarnated. If Christians are right, we will all stand before the judgment seat of God. If atheists are right, all of our existences will come to an end. If spiritists are right we'll all float around as ghosts. But they simply can't all be true at the same time.

So it's clear that there is such a thing as real truth that exists whatever individuals may choose to believe.

Tactic 3: Not Replacing Core Beliefs

All of us were raised wearing a virtual reality headset of one kind or another — it's our original worldview. But it's crucial to understand that these headsets give us a distorted view of reality.

The third tactic of the world is to get us to **add** our Christian beliefs to our existing worldview rather than **replace** the existing worldview so that our core beliefs remain the same.

Gold leaf is real gold that is beaten until it is 200 times thinner than a human hair, then it is applied to books, ornaments, buildings, and sometimes even food. Something that is covered in gold leaf looks as if it is made from solid gold but it's actually just a thin covering.

Imagine your Christian beliefs as a beautiful gold ornament. If we were to take a saw and cut it in half, what would you see inside? Would it be solid gold all the way through? Or would there just be a thin layer of gold with some cheap and nasty metal inside?

How are those brought up in the West affected by the Western worldview which in effect denies the reality of the spiritual world?

It encourages us to live our lives and exercise our ministries as if the spiritual world didn't exist. When something goes horribly wrong in our lives, many Christians blame God because, influenced by the Western worldview, they leave Satan out of the equation who, the Bible says, is a thief who "comes only to steal and kill and destroy" (John 10:10).

What about when someone has a mental or psychological problem? The medical profession, influenced by the Western worldview, tends to ignore the reality of the spiritual world and does not even acknowledge the possibility that an issue may have a spiritual cause.

We are whole people — spirit, soul, and body — and we need to take into account both the natural world and the spiritual world.

We say we believe the Bible, but are our decisions made on the basis of what we think rather than on what God is saying? We say we believe in the power of prayer but do our actions really demonstrate that we believe that we can sort out our lives ourselves and use prayer only as a last resort?

Consider this question: Why are you a Christian? Christians who are still operating according to their old worldview might say something like: "I believe because it seems to work"; or "I feel it is true in my experience"; or "I sincerely believe it is true for me."

But what happens when it no longer seems to work or when it doesn't feel true any more, or when another attractive belief system comes along?

Each of us needs to come to a point where we realize that what the world has caused us to believe is so contrary to what is really true that we make a conscious decision to throw it away. We need to make a conscious choice to believe what the Bible says, to make the Word of God our core belief system — not just something we add on like a coating of gold leaf to a faulty belief system.

If we don't, it will lead us to compromise and we'll be "double-minded" and "unstable in all our ways" (James 1:8).

REFLECTION

Spend some time in prayer throwing out your old worldview and choosing to see the world as God says it actually is.

You might find it helpful to say "I renounce the lie that [my old false belief], and I announce the truth that [truth from God's Word]," for example:

"I renounce the lie that the unseen spiritual world is not real, and I announce the truth that it is just as real as the physical world we can see."

"I renounce the lie that financial success brings real security, and I announce the truth that I am already perfectly secure because no one can snatch me out of God's hand."

"I renounce the lie that I should be worried that someone may have cursed me, and I announce the truth that I am seated with Christ in the heavenly realms far above all other spiritual powers."

 WITNESS

How will understanding that we all grow up with a particular way of looking at the world help you as you talk to people who are not yet Christians?

 IN THE COMING WEEK

At the end of each day take five minutes to review how your old worldview has reared its head during the day to try to persuade you to compromise the truth of the Bible. When you identify it happening, take time to renounce the false belief from your previous worldview and make a commitment to base your life on the truth of the Bible.

Our Daily Choice

 **WHAT'S IT ABOUT?**

OBJECTIVE: To understand that, although we still have urges that tend to pull us away from relying completely on God and following the promptings of His Spirit, we no longer have to give in to them but are free to make a genuine choice.

FOCUS VERSE: You, however, are not in the flesh but in the Spirit, if in fact the Spirit of God dwells in you. (Romans 8:9a ESV)

FOCUS TRUTH: Although you are a new person in Christ with a completely new nature, and are free to live according to what the Holy Spirit tells you, obeying Him is not automatic.

The second book in the FREEDOM IN CHRIST DISCIPLESHIP SERIES, *Win The Daily Battle*, corresponds to Part B of the course. Read pages 84–111 in the book for the material that relates to the flesh.

Steve Goss has put an additional short teaching session on the app called "Who Is Responsible For What?" that goes well with this session. We recommend that you watch it in the next week.

 WELCOME
What would you most like to do if you knew you could not fail?

 WORSHIP
Worship Him for who He is.
Hebrews 13:15, Revelation 19:5, Psalm 99:9, 1 Chronicles 29:11–13.

WORD

We might think that becoming a Christian means that we will automatically do everything right. But it doesn't work that way. As believers we sense the Holy Spirit deep down inside and we want to please God. But we often fail to live the Christian life in the way we want to, and sometimes we don't feel different at all. Our bad habits don't instantly disappear. In fact, the struggle with sin may seem to intensify. Why?

In this session we're going to look at what the Bible calls "the flesh," the second of our enemies.

> For those who live according to the flesh set their minds on the things of the flesh, but those who live according to the Spirit set their minds on the things of the Spirit. For to set the mind on the flesh is death, but to set the mind on the Spirit is life and peace. For the mind that is set on the flesh is hostile to God. (Romans 8:5–7a)

What Changed When We Became Christians?

We've already seen that the moment we became Christians, some dramatic changes took place.

We Have A New Heart And A New Spirit Within Us

One of the great prophecies of the Old Testament is this: "I will give you a new heart and put a new spirit within you" (Ezekiel 36:26). Before we were Christians our hearts were "deceitful . . . and beyond cure" (Jeremiah 17:9) — but now in Christ we have brand new clean hearts!

We Have New Life "In Christ"

We are new creations and are now alive in Christ.

We Have A New Master

Our new spiritual authority is God; before our conversion it was Satan (John 8:44).

What Did Not Change When We Became Christians?

Our Body Did Not Change

Physically we still look the same as before. One day we'll get a new body but, for now, we still have the same old flesh and bones.

Our "Flesh" Wasn't Taken Away

When we talk about the term "flesh" we are not referring to our physical bodies but talking about the urges and desires it has. You could think of the flesh as "the urge to do what comes naturally to a fallen human being."

As we grew up, independent of God, we learned to react, cope, and think in certain ways. These old ways of thinking and behaving are the primary characteristics of the flesh. When we became Christians no one pressed a "clear" button in our minds.

"Flesh" is an unfamiliar word, but it is a literal translation of the Greek word used in the New Testament which describes meat you would buy from the supermarket or the flesh that makes up your body.

Many modern Bible translations went through a phase where they didn't translate the word "flesh" literally but interpreted it as "sinful nature." That is understandable because the word "flesh" sounds old-fashioned. However, using the term "nature" could lead to confusion because, as we have seen, Christians do not any longer have a sinful nature but are "holy ones" who share God's nature (2 Peter 1:4).

Sin Did Not Die

How can we defeat sin? The bad news is we can't. The good news is that Christ has already done it for us! Sin itself is not dead. In fact, it is still extremely appealing, and it tempts us every day to try to meet our legitimate needs for security acceptance, and significance, through things other than God.

Then what has to change so that we don't go round in circles falling into the same old sin patterns?

It won't happen by trying harder. The key to freedom is knowing the truth. We need to know the truth about sin.

Even though sin used to be our master, Paul tells us that it has no power over us any more. Even though sin is very much alive, Paul tells us that we are to realize that we are alive to God and dead to sin (Romans 6:11). When we died with Christ, His death ended our relationship with sin.

Paul said in Romans 7:21 "So I find this law at work: although I want to do good, evil is right there with me." What is this law? Paul calls it the "law of sin" (Romans 7:23).

How do you overcome the law of sin that is still in effect? By a greater law. Romans 8:2 says "Through Christ Jesus the law of the Spirit of life set me free from the law of sin and death."

The law of the Spirit of life that's now at work in me as a child of God is far greater than the law of sin and death. Before I became a child of God, a saint, a holy one, I had no choice but to stay on the ground in my sin, but now in Christ I have the power to choose to fly above the law of sin and death!

PAUSE FOR THOUGHT 1

What are some of the main things that you notice have changed in you since you became a Christian? And what do you wish would have changed but hasn't?

In what particular type of situation do you recognize that you become more vulnerable to the attempts of the flesh to draw you toward sin? What practical steps can you put in place to help you at those times?

God's Word tells us that we are alive to Christ and dead to sin. Why does this not feel true some days? How can we rise above "the law of sin"?

Our Choices

We face some very real choices:

- even though we no longer have to think and react according to our flesh, we can choose to do so
- even though sin has no power over us, we can choose to give in to it

Three Different Types Of Person (1 Corinthians 2:14–3:3)

The Natural Person — 1 Corinthians 2:14 & Ephesians 2:1–3

This describes someone who is not yet a Christian:

- physically alive but spiritually dead
- separated from God
- living independently from God
- lives in the flesh; actions and choices dictated by the flesh (see Galatians 5:19–21)

The Spiritual Person — 1 Corinthians 2:15

The normal state for a Christian:

- has been transformed through faith in Christ
- spirit is now united with God's Spirit
- has received forgiveness, acceptance into God's family, realization of worth in Christ
- receives impetus from God's Spirit instead of the flesh
- is renewing the mind (getting rid of old patterns of thinking and replacing them with truth)
- emotions marked by peace and joy instead of turmoil
- chooses to walk in the Spirit and therefore demonstrates the fruit of the Spirit (see Galatians 5:22–23)
- still has the flesh but crucifies it daily as they recognize the truth that they are now dead to sin (see Romans 6:11–14)

The Fleshly Person — 1 Corinthians 3:3

A Christian who has been made spiritually alive but, instead of choosing to follow the impulses of the Spirit, follows the impulses of the flesh. Their daily life tends to mimic that of the natural (non-Christian) person rather than the spiritual person:

- mind occupied by wrong thoughts
- overwhelmingly negative emotions
- body showing signs of stress
- living in opposition to their identity in Christ
- feelings of inferiority, insecurity, inadequacy, guilt, worry, and doubt
- tendency to get "stuck" in certain sins (Romans 7:15–24)

Paul describes being stuck in sin-confess cycles as "miserable" or "wretched." Because our spirit is joined to God's Spirit, in our inner being we delight in God's law — we really want to go His way. Yet we find that we fail time and again. Maybe we return time and again to comfort eating or gossip or sexual sin. In the end we feel completely hopeless and conclude (wrongly) that we can never escape.

The salvation of fleshly Christians is not the issue. It's a question of how fruitful they will be.

Barriers To Growth

If you feel you are more of a fleshly person than a spiritual person right now, don't beat yourself up. God still loves you just as much and you are still a holy one. Just start to deal with the barriers that are holding you back.

Deception

As fleshly patterns of thinking get more and more ingrained, they become entrenched and we refer to them as "strongholds." They stop us seeing things as they really are and keep us in deception. Common areas of deception for the Christian would include thoughts like:

"This might work for others, but my case is different and it won't work for me."

"I could never have faith like so-and-so."

"God could never use me."

It takes a determined effort to deal with a stronghold and we'll show you how to do that in Session 8.

Unresolved Personal And Spiritual Conflicts

In Ephesians 4:26–27 Paul says:

> "In your anger do not sin": Do not let the sun go down while you are still angry, and do not give the devil a foothold.

In other words, if we do not deal with something like anger quickly and we let it turn into the sins of bitterness and unforgiveness, we give the devil a foothold, an opportunity to hold us back.

For example, if you have never truly forgiven someone who hurt you, you are leaving a big door open to the enemy to confuse your thinking and stop you from connecting with truth. If you do not close that door by obeying God and forgiving that person, no matter how well someone preaches the truth to you, you are unlikely ever really to get hold of it in a way that you can grasp and put into practice.

It's straightforward to get rid of the foothold. You will have the opportunity later in the course to go through a process called *The Steps to Freedom In Christ* which is a tool you can use to examine all the areas of your life and ask the Holy Spirit to show you where you have not repented and closed the door to the enemy's influence. You can then, in a controlled and calm way, take the authority you now have in Christ to repent of those things and cut off the capacity of the enemy to confuse your thinking. In our experience there is no Christian that does not benefit from this process and, for many, it's the key to getting hold of the truths that we are teaching in their heart, not just their head.

Not Assuming Responsibility For Our Lives

A final reason that we may not make progress is that we haven't learned to take responsibility for the things that God says are our responsibility.

Peter says, "His divine power has given us [past tense] everything [not **nearly** everything] we need for a godly life" (2 Peter 1:3). Paul agrees and says we already have "**every** spiritual blessing" (Ephesians 1:3).

So it's not a question of asking God to do something more. And it's not a question of looking for an anointed person to "zap" us or pray the "right" prayer.

It comes down to knowing just who you are: a holy child of the living God who already has everything they need to be the person God is calling them to be. And then understanding how to put it all into practice, which is what this course is all about.

NOTE: Steve Goss has put an additional short teaching session on the app ("Who Is Responsible For What?") that gives further help with this.

PAUSE FOR THOUGHT 2

How do you identify with the descriptions of the three different types of people that are mentioned in 1 Corinthians 2:14–3:3?

How have the barriers to growth mentioned caused you to show more of the characteristics of a "fleshly person" than a "spiritual person"?

What practical steps and daily choices can we put in place to ensure we act as a "spiritual person"?

Choosing To Walk By The Spirit Every Day

Once we've committed ourselves to believe the truth no matter what we feel, and once we've dealt with our unresolved spiritual conflicts, we are genuinely free to make a choice every day. We are back in the position Adam and Eve were in before the Fall, able to choose freely. That free will is hugely important to God.

Paul wrote, "Live by the Spirit, and you will not gratify the desires of the flesh" (Galatians 5:16).

The key choice we can make every day is whether to obey the promptings of the flesh or the promptings of the Holy Spirit. The two are in direct opposition to each other.

What Is Walking By The Spirit?

Walking By The Spirit Is Not:

Just A Good Feeling

Sometimes the Holy Spirit touches us in such a way that we feel full of joy or peace. That's a lovely gift when it happens, but being filled with the Spirit day-by-day is much more than that. Because if we base our life on having a good feeling, we'll always be looking for "the key" to feeling better and we'll be constantly chasing after a new experience. I've known so many people in our churches addicted to having other people pray for them. They seek a warm tingly feeling inside, or a cathartic emotional release. But there's no fruit in their lives until they realize they are responsible for their own growth in the Lord.

A License To Do Whatever We Want

Some think that freedom means we can cast off all the guidelines God has given to help us lead responsible lives. You can try that, and your sin of choice might feel like freedom for a short while, but eventually you realize it's actually bondage. The key question is: can you stop? If you can't, you have become a slave to sin.

Legalism (Slavishly Obeying A Set Of Rules)

The Old Testament law revealed the moral nature of God but nobody could live up to it. The point of the law was to lead us to Christ by teaching us how much we need Him (Galatians 3:24).

But Paul says, "If you are led by the Spirit, you are not under the law" (Galatians 5:18).

When we see living for God as obeying a set of rules or behaving in a certain way, our walk with Him becomes a joyless trudge. It's hard to keep it up, and very tempting to give up. God isn't blessed by people who obey because they feel they have to. He wants us to obey because we want to, because we delight in doing His will.

Walking By The Spirit Is:

True Freedom

Where the Spirit of the Lord is, there is freedom. (2 Corinthians 3:17)

The devil can't make you walk in the flesh, although he will try to draw you that way. We have the freedom to be the people God created us to be and to make the choice to live by faith in the power of the Holy Spirit.

Being Led

"My sheep listen to my voice; I know them, and they follow me." (John 10:27)

In New Testament times, sheep were not driven from behind but willingly followed the shepherd.

Walking At God's Pace In The Right Direction

"Come to me, all you who are weary and burdened, and I will give you rest. Take my yoke upon you and learn from me, for I am gentle and humble in heart, and you will find rest for your souls. For my yoke is easy and my burden is light." (Matthew 11:28–30)

Being yoked to Jesus doesn't work if only one of us is pulling. Nothing will get done if we expect God to do it all. And neither can we accomplish anything lasting for eternity by ourselves. Only Jesus knows the right pace and the right direction to walk. When we walk with Him we learn that His ways are not hard and we find rest for our souls.

How Can We Tell If We Are Walking By The Spirit?

Just as you can tell a tree by its fruit, you can tell whether you are walking by the Spirit by the fruit of your life.

If you're being led by the Spirit, your life will be increasingly marked by love, joy, peace, patience, kindness, goodness, faithfulness, gentleness, and self-control (Galatians 5:22–23).

If you are living according to your flesh, that too will be evident in your life (Galatians 5:19–21).

Perhaps you have become aware during this session that you are living according to the flesh. What is the appropriate response? Simply to confess it, deal with any footholds of the enemy, invite the Holy Spirit to fill you, and start obeying the promptings of the Spirit rather than the flesh.

Walking by the Spirit is a moment-by-moment, day-by-day experience. You can choose every moment of every day either to walk by the Spirit or to walk by the flesh.

REFLECTION

Paul said this to his younger disciple, Timothy:

> For this reason I remind you to fan into flame the gift of God, which is in you through the laying on of my hands. For the Spirit God gave us does not make us timid, but gives us power, love and self-discipline. (2 Timothy 1:6–7)

Who was responsible for "fanning into flame" the gift of the Holy Spirit in Timothy's life, God, Paul, or Timothy?

Whose responsibility is it to do that in your life? What are some of the ways you could do that?

Take some time on your own in prayer to commit to walk by the Spirit rather than the flesh and to fan into flame the gift of the Holy Spirit in your life.

WITNESS

How would you explain to a not-yet-Christian the benefits of being filled with the Spirit in a way that would make sense to them?

IN THE COMING WEEK

Every day specifically commit yourself to walk by the Spirit and ask the Holy Spirit to fill you.

The Battle For Our Minds

WHAT'S IT ABOUT?

OBJECTIVE: To understand that, although our enemy, the devil, is constantly attempting to get us to believe lies, we don't have to believe every thought that comes into our head but can hold each one up against truth and choose to accept or reject it.

FOCUS VERSE: Put on the full armor of God, so that you can take your stand against the devil's schemes. (Ephesians 6:11)

FOCUS TRUTH: We are all in a spiritual battle. It's a battle between truth and lies, and it takes place in our minds. If we are aware of how Satan works, we will not fall for his schemes.

> The second book in the FREEDOM IN CHRIST DISCIPLESHIP SERIES, *Win The Daily Battle*, corresponds to Part B of the course. Read pages 43–110 in the book for the material that relates to this session.
>
> Steve Goss has put an extra teaching film on the app called "Overcoming Temptation" that would be helpful to watch after this session.

WELCOME

Has anyone ever played a really good trick on you, or have you played one on someone else? What was it?

WORSHIP

His authority — our authority. Colossians 2:15, 20, Luke 10:19, Matthew 28:18–20, Ephesians 6:11–18.

WORD

The Battle Is Real

We're not just up against the world and the flesh but also against the devil, whom Jesus calls the "father of lies" (John 8:44). The good news is that Jesus came to destroy the devil's work (1 John 3:8).

The tendency of those of us brought up with the Western worldview is to run our lives as if the spiritual world did not exist. But from the beginning of Genesis to the end of Revelation, there's one continuous theme in the Bible: the battle between the kingdom of light and the kingdom of darkness; between the Spirit of Truth and the father of lies; between the Christ and the Antichrist.

We are in the battle whether we like it or not. Paul tells us explicitly that we are not fighting flesh and blood but "the spiritual forces of wickedness in the heavenly realms" (see Ephesians 6:10–18).

If we don't understand that we are in a battle or how that battle works, we're very likely to become a casualty — to be "neutralized" in our walk with the Lord.

Satan The Deceiver

When God created Adam and Eve to rule over the world the devil had to crawl at their feet in the form of a snake.

But when they sinned, Adam and Eve effectively handed over their right to rule the world to Satan. That's why Jesus referred to him as "the prince [or ruler] of this world" (John 12:31). He's also called "the ruler of the kingdom of the air" (Ephesians 2:2), and we're told that the whole world lies in his power (1 John 5:19).

Satan Is Not Like God

God and Satan are not equal and opposite powers or anything remotely like that, though Satan would like you to think that they are. The Bible makes a huge distinction between the "Creator" and the "created" (see John 1:3). Like us, Satan is a mere created being.

Satan Can Only Be In One Place At One Time

Because of that, we can infer that he can only be in one place at one time. He rules this world through "rulers, authorities, powers and spiritual forces of evil in the heavenly realms" (Ephesians 6:12), different types or levels of fallen angels. The Bible doesn't bother telling us a huge amount about how they are organized because we don't really need to know.

Only God is everywhere at once.

Satan's Power And Authority Do Not Even Begin To Compare To God's

At the Cross Jesus completely disarmed Satan (see Colossians 2:15) and Satan can only operate within the boundaries that God sets (see Jude 1:6). He can't just walk into your life and inflict damage and destruction.

Satan Does Not Know Everything

Every occult practice relates to the mind or the future, but Satan knows neither perfectly.

There's no evidence that Satan can read your mind. For example, all interaction in the Bible between angels and people or demons and people is done out loud.

In Daniel 2 God gave King Nebuchadnezzar some dreams. He demanded that his magicians told him what they meant but first they also had to tell him the content of his dreams. These sorcerers could not do it because their normal sources of power and information were demons and they clearly were unable to read the king's mind. If they had been able to, they would because that would have prevented Daniel from advancing in the king's service.

Satan does not know the future except what God has revealed.

Now that does not mean that Satan cannot put thoughts into your mind, something that the Bible clearly teaches he can do.

How Satan Works
By Putting Thoughts Into Our Mind

The Spirit clearly says that in later times some will abandon the faith and follow deceiving spirits and things taught by demons. (1 Timothy 4:1)

Three examples that show how we can be affected without even knowing it:

Satan rose up against Israel and incited David to take a census of Israel. (1 Chronicles 21:1)

Would David have done this if he had thought it was Satan's idea? Of course not! David believed that it was his own idea — even though the Bible makes clear that it wasn't.

The evening meal was being served, and the devil had already prompted Judas Iscariot, son of Simon, to betray Jesus. (John 13:2)

Weren't these Judas' own thoughts? No. The Bible clearly says that the thought came from the devil. And when Judas realized the implications of what he had done, he went out and hanged himself.

Then Peter said, "Ananias, how is it that Satan has so filled your heart that you have lied to the Holy Spirit and have kept for yourself some of the money you received for the land?" (Acts 5:3)

Ananias almost certainly thought that this was his own idea, but the Bible makes clear that it originated with Satan. Ananias was deceived and it had terrible consequences — God struck him dead. He sent a powerful message to the early Church about the importance of not compromising the truth.

If Satan can put thoughts into our mind, he can make them sound like our own. He probably would not choose to announce the thought with an evil cackle. No, he would make it sound like your own thought: "I'm useless, I'm ugly." Not every thought that comes into your mind is your own.

PAUSE FOR THOUGHT 1

Does the devil seem more or less powerful than you had imagined? In what ways?

"Not every thought that comes into your head is your own" (for example, "I'm useless," or "I'm dirty"). What do you think about this?

Looking back, can you identify occasions when a thought you have had may well have been from the enemy? Are those thoughts always completely false?

Through Temptation, Accusation, And Deception

Imagine your Christian life as a race, with the racetrack stretching out in front of you. Satan can't block the path or stop you from becoming everything that God wants you to be. All he can do is shout out to you from the sidelines.

He'll try to tempt you away ("Hey! Look what's over here! Come and get it. It'll make you feel better and no one needs to find out. You know you want to.").

Or he'll shout accusations at you ("You blew it again? You useless excuse for a Christian! You might as well sit down and give up.").

He'll also tell you barefaced lies ("Excuse me — you're going the wrong way. The finishing line is back that way.").

Satan is trying to get us into sin, to establish negative patterns of thought ("I'm hopeless" or "I'll never be able to") and to deceive us into worldly ways of thinking ("I can sort this out on my own" or "All I need is positive thinking").

The most defeated Christians believe the lies and sit down — "Yeah, you're right, it's hopeless." Others stand while they argue with the thoughts, but they make no progress. Victorious Christians simply ignore them. They take every thought captive to the obedience of Christ and keep running toward the finishing line.

Deception is Satan's primary strategy because if you are deceived, by definition you don't know it.

By Getting Footholds In Our Lives Through Sin

In the last session we looked at Ephesians 4:26–27 which says that if we don't deal with anger quickly, we give the devil a foothold in our life.

You can see the same principle in 2 Corinthians 2:10–11:

> Anyone you forgive, I also forgive. And what I have forgiven — if there was anything to forgive — I have forgiven in the sight of Christ for your sake, in order that Satan might not outwit us. For we are not unaware of his schemes.

Satan's greatest access to our lives is often through the sin of unforgiveness.

If Satan can lead us into sin, he gains a point of influence in our lives that he can use to hold us back, as if we are on a piece of elastic.

There is an extra film on the app, "Overcoming Temptation" that you might find useful at this point in the course.

The Relationship Between Demons And Christians

At the center of your being, your spirit is connected to God's spirit and Satan can't have you back. You have been purchased by the blood of the Lamb (1 Peter 1:18–19). In other words, we're not talking here about ownership or "possession."

But if we fall for Satan's temptation, accusation, or deception, he may gain a degree of influence in our minds (1 Peter 5:8). His goal is to neutralise us or even use us to further his agenda (for example, in Acts 5:3).

We read in 2 Corinthians 4:4 that Satan "has blinded the minds of unbelievers" and these footholds seem to work in believers in much the same way. They cause a degree of spiritual blindness and make it more difficult for us to "connect" with truth. That's why good teaching on its own isn't enough for us to grow. We may simply be unable to connect with it until we deal with these footholds of the enemy.

The good news is that getting rid of these footholds is not difficult or dramatic, and you'll get an opportunity to do that in a gentle and controlled way when we go through *The Steps To Freedom In Christ*. Many find that they are then able to grasp the truth of God's Word in a completely new way.

PAUSE FOR THOUGHT 2

"If you are deceived, by definition you don't know it." What are some of the ways that you might become aware of deception in your life?

What practical steps can you take to "take every thought captive" to obey Christ (2 Corinthians 10:5)?

If we have given the enemy a foothold through sin, how can we take that foothold away according to James 4:7?

Our Defense
Understand Our Position In Christ

Ephesians 1:19–22 says that Jesus is seated at God's right hand, the ultimate seat of power and authority, "far above all rule and authority, power and dominion." God has placed all things under His feet and we are told that He is now "head over **everything**" (our emphasis).

So what is our position?

Ephesians 2:6 says, "And God raised us up with Christ and seated us with Him in the heavenly realms in Christ Jesus."

We are seated with Jesus, **far** above Satan and all demonic powers. Not just slightly above!

Use The Resources We Have In Christ

Now even though Satan is defeated, he still "prowls around, like a roaring lion looking for someone to devour" (1 Peter 5:8).

However, James 4:7 says, "Submit to God. Resist the devil and he will flee from you." As long as you are submitting to God when you resist the devil he has no choice but to flee. This applies to every Christian no matter how weak and frail you feel, or how long or how short a time you have been a Christian. Every believer has the same authority and power in Christ over the spiritual world.

Do Not Be Frightened

There's nothing big about a demon except its mouth! They are like dogs with a big bark but no teeth. Demons are petrified of Christians who understand the magnitude of power and authority they have in Christ. Satan and demons have no power over Christians except what we give them.

What is the best response to the fact that there are demons all around? Simply to fix our eyes on Jesus and by faith live a righteous life in the power of the Holy Spirit. The last thing you need to do is go looking for a demon behind every bush.

However, the danger comes for those Christians who don't realize that demons are there, don't understand how they work, and don't know how to protect themselves.

> The one who was born of God keeps him safe, and the evil one cannot harm him. (1 John 5:18)

Guard Our Minds

We need to be careful what we allow into our minds.

There are a lot of Eastern influences coming into the business world, schools, and even churches that are spiritually dangerous. Often they want us to put our minds "into neutral."

> Search me, God, and know my heart; test me and know my anxious thoughts. See if there is any offensive way in me. (Psalm 139:23–24)

It's good to invite God to search our heart. However, we are never told to direct our thoughts inward or passively but always outward and actively. Even in 1 Corinthians 14, the definitive chapter on tongues and prophecy, Paul says if you pray with your spirit, you should also pray with your mind.

God does not bypass our minds — He works through them.

Turn On The Light

Some people are concerned to know whether the thoughts in their mind are from the enemy or not. That's the wrong question. The real issue is not where the thought came from but whether it's true! We are told to, "take **every** thought captive." (2 Corinthians 10:5). Whether it comes from your memory, the TV, the internet, or a deceiving spirit, if it is not true, don't believe it!

Do we need to keep checking our thoughts and rebuking the enemy every five minutes to see if he has put a thought into our mind? No. If you're in a dark room and you want to see, you don't shoo the darkness away. No — you turn on the light! Don't focus on the enemy, focus on the truth.

Bank clerks are trained to recognize forged currency by studying the real thing. They get to know what real currency looks like so they are able to spot fake ones when they come through. In the same way, our defense against deception is to know the truth.

So let's not focus on the enemy. Instead, as Paul instructs:

> Whatever is true, whatever is noble, whatever is right, whatever is pure, whatever is lovely, whatever is admirable — if anything is excellent or praiseworthy — think about such things. (Philippians 4:8)

REFLECTION

"The One who was born of God keeps them safe, and the evil one cannot harm them" (1 John 5:18b). Spend a few minutes as a group discussing this powerful truth and how it applies to your daily life.

Read Ephesians 6:10–18 pausing after each element of the armor of God to pray. As you pray, visualize yourself putting on — or having on — each piece of the armor and commit yourself to what it represents, for example:

"I put on the belt of truth. I commit myself to believe the truth, speak only the truth, and live according to the truth."

"I thank You that Jesus has made me righteous and that the breastplate of righteousness covers my heart."

WITNESS

How do you think Satan works in the lives of your non-Christian friends? What might you be able to do about this?

 IN THE COMING WEEK

Meditate on the following verses: Matthew 28:18; Ephesians 1:3–14; Ephesians 2:6–10; Colossians 2:13–15.

Part C

BREAKING THE HOLD OF THE PAST

God does not change our past but by His grace He enables us to walk free of it. This section of the course includes going through *The Steps To Freedom In Christ* (see separate booklet *The Steps To Freedom In Christ*).

Handling Emotions Well

WHAT'S IT ABOUT?

OBJECTIVE: To understand our emotional nature and how it is related to what we believe.

FOCUS VERSE: Cast all your anxiety on him because he cares for you. Be alert and of sober mind. Your enemy the devil prowls around like a roaring lion looking for someone to devour. (1 Peter 5:7–8)

FOCUS TRUTH: Our emotions are essentially a product of our thoughts and a barometer of our spiritual health.

The third book in the FREEDOM IN CHRIST DISCIPLESHIP SERIES, *Break Free, Stay Free*, corresponds to Part C of the course. Read pages 12–55 in the book for some key principles and the material that relates to this session.

WELCOME

Would you describe yourself as an emotional person? Tell the group about an event in the past that resulted in emotional pain or joy.

WORSHIP

He made us so well, and He knows us so well! Psalm 139.

WORD

The Bible Describes God Using Emotional Language

He loves us so much that He's described as "jealous" (Exodus 34:14).

We are told it is possible to "grieve" the Holy Spirit (Ephesians 4:30).

Jesus wept at the grave of Lazarus (John 11:35) and when He looked at Jerusalem (Luke 19:41).

We Can't Directly Control How We Feel

We are made in God's image so we too have an emotional nature.

We can't simply turn our emotions on and off with a remote control like we do our TV. Although you can't control them directly, you can change them over time, as you make a conscious choice to change what you choose to believe.

Negative Emotions — Our Red Warning Light

Your emotions are to your soul what your ability to feel pain is to your body.

If you go to the dentist for a filling and have an anaesthetic, you will usually be told not to eat anything for a while afterward. You may think that this is so you don't damage the filling. In fact it's not so much to protect the filling as to protect the soft tissue in your mouth such as your tongue and your cheeks. Eating with a numb mouth is dangerous. You are likely to mangle your tongue and cheeks as you chew because you can't feel a thing.

God gave us the ability to feel physical pain for our own protection.

If you had no ability to feel physical pain you would be a hopeless mass of scars within a matter of weeks.

Negative emotions perform this same function, but for your soul. Wouldn't it be great if you never felt depressed or anxious or angry? No it wouldn't.

You can think of negative emotions as being like that red warning light that comes on occasionally in your car. The light is there to alert you to a potentially serious problem in the engine.

Our natural reaction when a painful emotion appears can be to ignore it — but that's like taking a piece of tape to cover the warning light — "no problem, the light's gone away." Consciously ignoring our feelings or choosing not to deal with them is unhealthy. It's like trying to bury a live mole. It will eventually tunnel its way to the surface, usually in some other unhealthy way — maybe in the form of an illness.

Another way of dealing with the red light is to pick up a hammer and smash it. In other words, we simply explode in an outburst of anger. "That's better. I just had to get that off my chest" — but it can be devastating for your spouse, children, or whoever else is in the perimeter of explosion.

The most suitable response when that red light comes on, of course, is to stop and take a good look at the engine to see what the problem is. And that's the best way to handle negative emotions too. Their function is to alert you to a problem with what you believe.

If what you believe does not reflect what is actually true, then what you feel won't reflect reality.

In Lamentations 3:1–11 Jeremiah is in complete despair because he believes that God is the cause of all his problems.

> I am the man who has seen affliction by the rod of the LORD's wrath.
> He has driven me away and made me walk in darkness rather than light;
> indeed, he has turned his hand against me again and again, all day long.
> He has made my skin and my flesh grow old and has broken my bones.
> He has besieged me and surrounded me with bitterness and hardship.
> He has made me dwell in darkness like those long dead.
> He has walled me in so I cannot escape; he has weighed me down with chains.
> Even when I call out or cry for help, he shuts out my prayer.
> He has barred my way with blocks of stone; he has made my paths crooked.
> Like a bear lying in wait, like a lion in hiding, he dragged me from the path
> and mangled me and left me without help.

But look again at what Jeremiah believed. Is it true? Would God really turn His hand against one of His servants again and again? Does He surround His people with bitterness and hardship? Does He shut out our prayers? Of course not!

What was the problem? Simply that what Jeremiah believed about God wasn't actually true! God hadn't walled him in. God wasn't like a wild animal who had mangled him.

Thankfully, Jeremiah doesn't leave it there. He thinks more about it and has a change in perspective.

Lamentations 3:19–24:

> I remember my affliction and my wandering, the bitterness and the gall.
>
> I well remember them, and my soul is downcast within me.
>
> Yet this I call to mind and therefore I have hope:
>
> Because of the LORD's great love we are not consumed, for his compassions never fail.
>
> They are new every morning; great is your faithfulness.
>
> I say to myself, "The LORD is my portion; therefore I will wait for him."

What changed in his circumstances? Absolutely nothing. Did God change? No! The only thing that changed was in his mind: how he looked at his circumstances.

PAUSE FOR THOUGHT 1

Look at the example of Jesus in Matthew 26:37 and that of David in 2 Samuel 6:14. What can they teach us?

"God gave us the ability to feel emotional pain for our own protection." Do you agree? If so, how do you think that works in practice?

Discuss this statement: "If what you believe does not reflect what is actually true, then what you feel won't reflect reality."

Negative Emotions Can Help Us

Things like hormones or even the weather can play a part in producing negative emotions but generally speaking they are a gift from God to help us uncover something we believe that isn't actually true. Let's consider two areas where they do that.

1. Faulty Life-Goals

Firstly they can help us uncover faulty life-goals. We've seen how God created us to be accepted, significant, and secure.

Every day as we grew up, we saw our lives stretching out ahead of us and, whether we realized it or not, we got up and we worked toward whatever we thought would give us those things. Consciously or unconsciously we developed a set of "life-goals." But are those life-goals the same as the goals God has for us? Negative emotions can help us identify those that are not.

Anger Signals A Blocked Life-Goal

If you are finding yourself feeling angry a lot, it's usually because someone or something is blocking a goal you have.

Suppose you have consciously or unconsciously developed a life-goal to have a loving, harmonious, happy Christian family. Is that a good thing? Well, who can block that goal? Every person in the family! At the end of the day, you can only do so much to influence how your family turns out but you can't control every factor. If you have a belief that achieving this goal is what's going to make you significant, you will go to pieces every time your spouse or children fail to live up to your image of family harmony.

Anxiety Signals An Uncertain Life-Goal

Anxiety is signaling that achieving a goal feels uncertain. You are hoping something will happen, but you have no guarantee that it will. You can control some of the factors, but not all of them.

For example, if you have come to believe that your sense of security depends on financial success and that has become a life-goal, you will probably suffer from anxiety. Why? Because you have no guarantee that you can ever get enough money or, even if you feel you have enough, that it won't be wiped out by a financial crisis.

Depression Signals An Impossible Life-Goal

Sometimes a life-goal that was already uncertain seems to slip even further away to the point where its fulfillment begins to appear impossible: "It's never going to happen." At that point anxiety turns to depression.

Of course, the causes of depression are complex and our hormones and other things going on in our bodies can play a part. But if there is no overriding physical cause, then depression is usually rooted in a sense of hopelessness or helplessness. But no child of God is helpless and no child of God is hopeless, whatever their circumstances.

We will get rid of a great deal of anger, anxiety, and depression if we ensure that our life-goals are in line with God's goals for us. Any goal God has for us is one that will not be able to be blocked by other people or by circumstances that we have no right or ability to control. How can we be so sure? Because God loves us too much to set us a goal that we couldn't reach. In our final session we will work out what a healthy life-goal looks like.

2. Uncovering Lies That Past Experiences Have Taught Us To Believe

All of us have had traumatic experiences that have scarred us in some way. When you suffered that negative experience you mentally processed it at the time it happened. It almost certainly caused you to believe some things about God and yourself: for example, "Those bullies told me I was rubbish — I guess I am."

The beliefs that come as a result of those traumatic experiences can become deeply ingrained strongholds. We'll look at how to demolish them in Session 8 but for now let's just recognize this: we remain in bondage to the past, not because of the traumatic experience itself, but because of the lies it caused us to believe.

Children of God are not primarily products of their past. They are primarily products of Christ's work on the cross and His resurrection. Nobody can change our past, but we can choose to walk free of it. That's the whole point of the Gospel.

When Jesus was in the synagogue at Capernaum, He specifically turned to what we now know as Isaiah 61 and said "Today this is fulfilled in your presence." He was stating His mandate:

> "The Spirit of the Lord is on me,
> because he has anointed me
> to proclaim good news to the poor.
> He has sent me to proclaim freedom for the prisoners
> and recovery of sight for the blind,
> to set the oppressed free,
> to proclaim the year of the Lord's favor."
> (Luke 4:18–19)

Every Christian needs the Biblical principles in the *Freedom In Christ Course* but the wonderful thing is that they work for those with even the deepest hurts. Jesus didn't just come to give you a way to **cope** with the effects of the past. He came to help you **resolve** those effects completely. It takes time and it's a struggle. But He is with you every step and He's already given you everything you need.

PAUSE FOR THOUGHT 2

Describe a life-goal you have had that you thought would make you feel significant, secure, and accepted that ended up being "blocked."

How can traumatic experiences lead us to believe a lie about ourselves, God, or Satan?

Discuss this statement: "Children of God are not primarily products of their past. They are primarily products of Christ's work on the cross and His resurrection. Nobody can change our past, but we can choose to walk free of it. That's the whole point of the Gospel. "

The Dangers

We saw in the last session how the emotion of anger can give the enemy a foothold in our lives if we don't quickly resolve an offense. Anxiety has similar dangers.

Here's a verse you probably know: "Cast all your anxiety on him because he cares for you." And here's another one: "Be alert and of sober mind. Your enemy the devil prowls around like a roaring lion looking for someone to devour."

What you many not know is that these verses directly follow each other in 1 Peter 5:7–8. They are both part of the same idea. Peter is telling us to be self-controlled and not let anxiety take hold of us. If we don't, he warns that the devil, like a roaring lion, is prowling around looking to devour us.

Three Keys To Emotional Health

Know Who You Are In Christ

If you know your true identity in Christ — in your heart, not just your head — you won't go looking for acceptance, significance, and security in those faulty life-goals.

And those who have suffered trauma in the past, you can learn to re-evaluate your past experiences from the perspective of who you now are in Christ.

The truth is you are a complete, clean, holy child of God with unlimited potential in Him. You might be thinking, "But I had awful things done to me that make me feel dirty." That doesn't change who you are now. You may feel dirty but you are not actually dirty because you are a new creation in Christ. As you understand and believe this truth — and forgive those who have hurt you from your heart — you can walk in your freedom in Christ.

Be Honest

Psalm 109:6–15:

Appoint someone evil to oppose my enemy; let an accuser stand at his right hand. When he is tried, let him be found guilty, and may his prayers condemn him. May his days be few; may another take his place of leadership. May his children be fatherless and his wife a widow. May his children be wandering beggars; may they be driven from their ruined homes. May a creditor seize all he has; may strangers plunder the fruits of his labor. May no one extend kindness to him or take pity on his fatherless children. May his descendants be cut off, their names blotted out from the next generation. May the iniquity of his fathers be remembered before the Lord; may the sin of his mother never be blotted out. May their sins always remain before the Lord that he may cut off the memory of them from the earth.

Have you ever felt like that? Have you ever prayed like that? Would it be right to pray like that? Well, David prayed like that, and God inspired him to write it down.

Does God already know you feel that way? Of course He does. God knows the thoughts and intentions of our hearts.

So the question is, if God already knows it, why can't we be honest with Him? Would He still love us if we were totally honest with Him about how we feel? Absolutely!

You can be completely honest with God. He is your closest friend. As a matter of fact, you can't be right with God without first being real with Him. God may use the circumstances of your life to make you real in order that you can be right with Him.

Commit To Believing The Truth

Our freedom comes from knowing the truth.

If you realize that you have had a faulty understanding of God, reading the "My Father God" list out loud every day for six weeks or so can dramatically help heal your emotional pain.

WITNESS

If you are feeling angry, anxious, or depressed, do you think it would be better not to let that show to not-yet-Christians around you? Why? Why not?

 IN THE COMING WEEK

Consider the emotional nature of the Apostle Peter. First, have a look at some occasions where he let his emotions run away with him and acted or spoke too hastily: Matthew 16:21–23; Matthew 17:1–5; John 18:1–11. Second, look at how Jesus was able to look beyond these emotional outbursts and see his potential: Matthew 16:17–19. Finally, see how that came true when Peter, under the power of the Holy Spirit, became the spokesperson of the early church: Acts 2:14–41. Nothing in your character is so big that God cannot make something good out of it!

My Father God

I renounce the lie that You, Father God, are distant and uninterested in me.

I choose to believe the truth that You, Father God, are always personally present with me, have plans to give me a hope and a future, and have prepared works in advance specifically for me to do. (Psalm 139:1–18; Matthew 28:20, Jeremiah 29:11, Ephesians 2:10)

I renounce the lie that You, Father God, are insensitive and don't know me or care for me.

I choose to believe the truth that You, Father God, are kind and compassionate and know every single thing about me. (Psalm 103:8–14; 1 John 3:1–3; Hebrews 4:12–13)

I renounce the lie that You, Father God, are stern and have placed unrealistic expectations on me.

I choose to believe the truth that You, Father God, have accepted me and are joyfully supportive of me. (Romans 5:8–11; 15:17)

I renounce the lie that You, Father God, are passive and cold toward me.

I choose to believe the truth that You, Father God, are warm and affectionate toward me. (Isaiah 40:11; Hosea 11:3–4)

I renounce the lie that You, Father God, are absent or too busy for me.

I choose to believe the truth that You, Father God, are always present and eager to be with me and enable me to be all that You created me to be. (Philippians 1:6; Hebrews 13:5)

I renounce the lie that You, Father God, are impatient or angry with me or have rejected me.

I choose to believe the truth that You, Father God, are patient and slow to anger, and that when You discipline me, it is a proof of Your love, and not rejection. (Exodus 34:6; Romans 2:4; Hebrews 12:5–11)

I renounce the lie that You, Father God, have been mean, cruel, or abusive to me.

I choose to believe the truth that Satan is mean, cruel, and abusive, but You, Father God, are loving, gentle, and protective. (Psalm 18:2; Matthew 11:28–30; Ephesians 6:10–18)

I renounce the lie that You, Father God, are denying me the pleasures of life.

I choose to believe the truth that You, Father God, are the author of life and will lead me into love, joy, and peace when I choose to be filled with Your Spirit. (Lamentations 3:22–23; Galatians 5:22–24)

I renounce the lie that You, Father God, are trying to control and manipulate me.

I choose to believe the truth that You, Father God, set me free and gave me the freedom to make choices and grow in Your grace. (Galatians 5:1; Hebrews 4:15–16)

I renounce the lie that You, Father God, have condemned me and no longer forgive me.

I choose to believe the truth that You, Father God, have forgiven all my sins and will never use them against me in the future. (Jeremiah 31:31–34; Romans 8:1)

I renounce the lie that You, Father God, reject me when I fail to live a perfect or sinless life.

I choose to believe the truth that You, Father God, are patient toward me and cleanse me when I fail. (Proverbs 24:16; 1 John 1:7–2:2)

I AM THE APPLE OF YOUR EYE! (Deuteronomy 32:9–10)

Forgiving From The Heart

WHAT'S IT ABOUT?

OBJECTIVE: To recognize what forgiveness is and what it is not, and to learn how to forgive from the heart.

FOCUS VERSE: In anger his master turned him over to the jailers to be tortured, until he should pay back all he owed. This is how my heavenly Father will treat each of you unless you forgive your brother from your heart. (Matthew 18:34–35)

FOCUS TRUTH: In order to experience our freedom in Christ, we need to relate to other people in the same way that God relates to us — on the basis of complete forgiveness and acceptance.

> The third book in the FREEDOM IN CHRIST DISCIPLESHIP SERIES, *Break Free, Stay Free*, corresponds to Part C of the course. Pages 56–98 relate to *The Steps To Freedom In Christ* including forgiveness, the subject of this session (read pages 63–75 in the book for the specific material on forgiveness).

WELCOME
Read Matthew 18:21–35 or act it out using the script on pages 126–127. Then try to put yourself in the place of one of the characters and say what strikes you most about the story.

WORSHIP
His complete forgiveness of us. Hebrews 4:16, Ephesians 3:12, Psalm 130:1–5.

WORD

Why Forgive?

> Anyone you forgive, I also forgive. And what I have forgiven . . . I have forgiven in
> the sight of Christ for your sake, in order that Satan might not outwit us. For we
> are not unaware of his schemes. (2 Corinthians 2:10–11)

Nothing gives Satan greater opportunity to stop a church growing than bitterness
and division.

It Is Required By God (Matthew 6:9–15)

> This, then, is how you should pray: "Our Father in heaven, hallowed be your
> name, your kingdom come, your will be done on earth as it is in heaven. Give us
> today our daily bread. Forgive us our sins, as we also have forgiven those who
> have sinned against us." (Matthew 6:9–12 our own translation)

Your relationship with God is tied to your relationship with other people. You really
can't have a righteous relationship with God in isolation from your relationships
with other people.

> Whoever claims to love God yet hates a brother or sister is a liar. For whoever
> does not love their brother and sister, whom they have seen, cannot love God,
> whom they have not seen. (1 John 4:20)

God wants us to learn to relate to others on the same basis that He relates to us.

It Is

Essential For Our Freedom

The most definitive teaching on forgiveness is in Matthew 18:21–35:

> Then Peter came to Jesus and asked, "Lord, how many times shall I forgive my brother when he sins against me? Up to seven times?" Jesus answered, "I tell you, not seven times, but seventy-seven times."

Jesus isn't suggesting here that you keep tabs of each time someone offends you until you reach 78, then get a gun and blow their brains out! He's saying that you just continue to forgive. God doesn't want His children to languish in bitterness and be bound to the past.

The Extent Of Our Own Debt

In order to forgive this freely we need to understand, first of all, the extent of our own debt to God. In Luke 7:36–50 there is a contrast between Simon the Pharisee, who did not extend common courtesies to Jesus, and a woman who had lived a sinful life who slipped in uninvited. She began to wash Jesus' feet with her tears, wipe them with her hair, anoint His feet with oil and kiss them repeatedly which irritated Simon. Jesus said, "Those who have been forgiven much love much. Those who have been forgiven little love little."

How much have you been forgiven? Little or much? No matter how well we may think we've done, the truth is our best is like a dirty rag before God (Isaiah 64:6). Without Christ, we all stand condemned. We've all been forgiven much though we may not realize it. But if we do realize it, we'll find that our capacity for loving others will increase.

Repayment Is Impossible

Jesus continues in Matthew 18:

> Therefore, the kingdom of heaven is like a king who wanted to settle accounts with his servants. As he began the settlement, a man who owed him ten thousand [talents] was brought to him. Since he was not able to pay, the master ordered that he and his wife and his children and all that he had be sold to repay the debt.

> At this the servant fell on his knees before him. "Be patient with me," he begged, "and I will pay back everything."

Ten thousand talents was a huge sum, way beyond a lifetime's earnings — a seven figure sum in today's terms. What Jesus is trying to show by using such a large amount is that repayment is not an option. There was no way the servant could possibly repay the debt!

How big was your debt to God? Far too large for you ever to repay.

So if the servant is to sort this issue out, another way has to be found.

Mercy Is Required

The servant's master took pity on him, canceled the debt and let him go.

Justice is giving people what they deserve.
God is just, it's part of His character. If He gave us what we deserve, we would all get hell.

Thankfully God is also merciful and He found a way to forgive and accept us without compromising justice. The punishment we deserved fell at unimaginable cost on Christ.

Mercy is not giving people what they deserve.
We are told to be merciful to others as God has been merciful to us (Luke 6:36). But our generous God goes even further than that. He didn't just take our punishment on Himself so that we could go free. He actually showers us with good gifts that we don't deserve.

Grace is giving people what they don't deserve.
God set the standard by His own example. So He expects us to relate to other people in exactly the same way. We are not to give people the retribution they deserve. In fact we are to give them the forgiveness and blessings they don't deserve, which is what the master did for the servant and what Jesus has done for us. It all begins with the relationship that God has established with us: "Freely you have received, freely give" (Matthew 10:8).

PAUSE FOR THOUGHT 1

Why are people (including Christians) often unwilling to forgive?

In order to understand how important it is to forgive others, we need to understand how much we ourselves have been forgiven. Discuss this idea.

Look at the definitions of justice, mercy, and grace. How does God come to us when we go wrong? How can we go to other people in the same way?

So That No Advantage Can Be Taken Of You (2 Corinthians 2:10–11)

But when that servant went out, he found one of his fellow servants who owed him a hundred [denarii].

A denarius is a day's wages — so one hundred denarii is about three months' worth of income. That's not a small debt, but it was a lot less than the one he had been let off.

He grabbed him and began to choke him. "Pay back what you owe me!" he demanded. His fellow-servant fell to his knees and begged him, "Be patient with me, and I will pay you back."

But he refused. Instead, he went off and had the man thrown into prison until he could pay the debt. When the other servants saw what had happened, they were outraged and went and told their master everything that had happened. Then the master called the servant in. "You wicked servant," he said, "I canceled all that debt of yours because you begged me to. Shouldn't you have had mercy on your fellow servant just as I had on you?"

In anger his master turned him over to the jailers to be tortured, until he should pay back all he owed. This is how my heavenly Father will treat each of you unless you forgive your brother from your heart.

The word used for "torture" usually refers to spiritual torment in the New Testament. It is the same word the demon used in Mark 5:7 when the demon said to Jesus, "Swear to God that you won't torture me!"

Jesus warns us that if we don't forgive others from our heart, we will suffer some kind of spiritual torment. In other words, we are opening a door to bring the enemy's influence or spiritual attack into our life.

Forgiving From The Heart

To forgive someone from the heart means we have to be emotionally honest with God and ourselves and face the hurt and pain we feel. In *The Steps To Freedom In Christ* we use a simple but effective formula. You go to God and choose to be emotionally honest with Him by saying:

"Lord I choose to forgive [the person] for [say what they did or failed to do] because it made me feel [then tell God every hurt and pain you felt]."

We encourage people to stay with this process until every hurt that is uncovered has been put on the table. We have to let God lead us to the emotional core where healing is going to take place.

This is not easy and can be painful but we do it in order to completely resolve the pain that we have been carrying around. We can't move on from the past until we choose to forgive.

One of the key points we need to understand when it comes to forgiveness is that the real issue is not so much between us and the other person but between us and God because He is the one who commands us to forgive. We don't even have to go to the other person in order to forgive them. In fact, the process of forgiveness doesn't involve them at all — it is between us and God alone.

Yes, Jesus did say that if we go to church and remember that somebody has something against us, we should leave our offering and go and be reconciled with that person. If you have offended someone else, go to that person, ask for forgiveness and put things right as far as you are able. But if someone has offended you, don't go to them, go to God. Your need to forgive others is first and foremost an issue between you and God. If you think about it, there is logic in it: because your freedom cannot be dependent on other people — otherwise it could not be guaranteed.

After you have forgiven, you may or may not be reconciled to the other person. That doesn't depend just on you. But whether you are reconciled or not, you will have removed the enemy's ability to hold you back.

We Forgive To Stop The Pain

When you forgive, it is for your sake. You might be thinking, "But you don't know how much they hurt me." But don't you see that they are still hurting you? How do you stop the pain? By forgiving.

By choosing not to forgive someone for what they did, we stay hooked to the pain of what they did. We think that by forgiving someone, we let him or her off the hook — but, if we don't forgive, we're the ones with the hook in us.

Holding on to bitterness and unforgiveness is like swallowing poison and hoping the other person will die!

PAUSE FOR THOUGHT 2

What is your reaction to the idea that unforgiveness opens the door to the enemy's influence in your life?

"The longer you leave the hook in, the more pain it will cause you." Discuss.

What do you think about this statement: "When it comes to forgiveness, the real issue is not so much between us and the other person, it's between us and God"?

What Forgiveness Is And What It Isn't

Not Forgetting

You can't get rid of a hurt simply by trying to forget it.

You might say, "Well, doesn't God forget our sins?" God is all-knowing — He couldn't forget if He wanted to. When God says "I will remember their sins no more" (Jeremiah 31:34), what He is saying is, "I won't take the past and use it against you. I will put it away from me as far as the east is from the west." If a husband says to a wife, "I've forgiven you but remember, on January 10, 2013, you did this . . . ," do you know what he's actually saying? "I haven't forgiven you. I am still taking the past and using it against you." So part of that commitment to forgive is about deciding not to bring up the past and use it against them ever again.

Not Tolerating Sin

Forgiveness does not mean that we tolerate sin. Does God forgive? He does. Does He tolerate sin. No, He can't.

You have every right to put a stop to sin by laying down Biblical guidelines, or by removing yourself from a particular situation. That is not at all inconsistent with forgiveness. If you don't put an end to a cycle of abuse it will just continue.

Not Seeking Revenge

The main difficulty we have with forgiveness is that understandably we want revenge, we want justice.

We somehow think that forgiving means we just have to sweep it under the carpet and say it didn't matter. God says:

> Do not take revenge, my dear friends, but leave room for God's wrath, for it is written: "It is mine to avenge; I will repay," says the Lord. (Romans 12:19)

In no way is God asking you to sweep what was done under the carpet as if it did not matter. In fact quite the opposite. He promises that if you hand the matter over to Him, He will ensure that it is not swept under the carpet. When you forgive, although you are letting the person off your hook, you are not letting them off God's hook.

When you choose to forgive, you are taking a step of faith to trust God to be the righteous judge who will weigh what was done on the scales of justice and will demand that the scales balance. God really will demand full payment for everything done to you. Everyone who sinned against you will have to stand before God and explain it — either it will be paid for by the blood of Christ if the person is a Christian, or they will have to face the judgment of God if they are not. "I will repay" — God will settle every account some day.

You are choosing to take a step of faith and trust God with what happened, to hand all of that pain and those demands for justice and revenge over to Him safe in the knowledge that He will ensure that justice is done. In the meantime you can walk free of it.

Resolving To Live With The Consequences Of Another's Sin

Part of forgiving is agreeing to live with the consequences of someone else's sin. You may say, "Well, that's not fair." No it's not — but you will have to do it anyway. The only real choice we have is whether to do that in the bondage of bitterness or the freedom of forgiveness.

Conclusion

Forgiveness is to set a captive free and then realize that you were the captive!

This is an issue between you and God. He commands you to forgive because He loves you. He knows that bitterness will defile you and others, and cause you to miss out on the abundant life that Jesus came to give you and not become a fruitful disciple.

You may agonize about whether what the person did was really wrong or you might think of reasons to justify what they did. But that is to miss the point. The issue of forgiveness is not primarily about who was right and who was wrong. If you felt offended you need to forgive — regardless of any other circumstance.

You will have an opportunity to forgive when we go through *The Steps To Freedom In Christ*. There are some guidelines on pages 122–125 to prepare you for that.

REFLECTION

Spend some time praying together for those who have indicated they are ready and willing to forgive others when we go through *The Steps To Freedom In Christ*. (There is no need to share anything — just pray.)

Then discuss the following statements:
"Forgiving has little to do with the person who hurt you."
"Forgiving is not forgetting."
"God will ensure justice is done."

WITNESS

How might this question of forgiveness challenge someone who is not yet a Christian? Are there any ways you can demonstrate forgiveness to someone who does not yet know God?

IN THE COMING WEEK

Ask the Holy Spirit to prepare your heart by leading you into truth and starting to reveal to you the areas you will need to bring into the light when you go through *The Steps To Freedom In Christ*.

Steps To Forgiveness

1. Ask God to reveal to your mind the people you need to forgive

Make a list of everyone God brings to your mind. Ask the Holy Spirit to guide you and write the names on a separate piece of paper. Even if you think there is no one, just ask God to bring up all the right names. The two most overlooked names are yourself and God.

Forgiving yourself: Only God can forgive your sins — but for many people, especially perfectionists, the hardest person to forgive is themselves, for letting themselves down. You are in effect accepting God's forgiveness and refusing to listen to the devil's accusations. Some people are really helped by being able to say, "I forgive myself for [list everything you hold against yourself], and I let myself off my own hook."

Forgiving God: Forgiving God is harder to understand because God has done nothing wrong. He has always acted in your best interests. But because you have not understood God's larger plan, or because you have blamed God for something that other people or the devil have done, you may have felt that God has let you down.

Many people feel disappointed with God, even angry with Him, because He didn't answer their prayer; He didn't seem to be there for them. They cried out for help and nothing came. Usually they are embarrassed to admit it. But God knows anyway and He's big enough to handle it.

If you feel uncomfortable telling God you forgive Him, say something like, "I release the expectations, thoughts, and feelings I have had against You."

2. Acknowledge the hurt and the hate

Jesus instructed us to forgive from the heart. That's much more than simply saying "I forgive" and pretending we've dealt with it. To forgive from the heart we need to face the hurt and the hate. People try to suppress their emotional pain, but it is trying to surface so that we can let it go.

3. Understand the significance of the cross

The cross is what makes forgiveness legally and morally right. Jesus has already taken upon Himself your sins and the sins of the person who has hurt you. He died "once for all" (Hebrews 10:10). When your heart says, "It isn't fair," remember that the justice is in the cross.

4. Decide that you will bear the burden of each person's sin

You need to make a choice not to use the information you have against that person in the future.

"He who covers over an offense promotes love, but whoever repeats the matter separates close friends" (Proverbs 17:9). That doesn't mean that you never testify in a court of law — however, you do it not in the bitterness of unforgiveness but having first forgiven from your heart.

5. Decide to forgive

Forgiveness is a crisis of the will. If you wait until you feel like doing it, you probably never will. You may feel you can't do it — but would God really tell you to do something you couldn't do? When He says that you can do everything through Christ who gives you strength (Philippians 4:13), is that true or not? The reality is that you have a choice to make — are you going to remain in bitterness, hooked to the past, giving the enemy an entrance to your mind; or are you going to get rid of it once and for all?

You **choose** to forgive, and in making that choice you are agreeing to live with sin and its consequences. You are choosing to let God be the avenger, and trust Him to bring justice in the end. You choose to take it to the cross and leave it there.

The gates of hell can't prevail against the Kingdom of God. There is nobody out there keeping you from being the person that God created you to be. The only one that can do that is you. You need to forgive, be merciful, and love as Christ has loved you. Let that person go; get on with your life; walk away free in Christ.

6. Take your list to God

To forgive from your heart, say, for example, "Lord, I choose to forgive my father" and then specify what you are forgiving him for. Stay with the same person until you have told God every pain and hurt that has surfaced and be as specific as you can. It's then helpful to take it a step further and say how it made you feel: "I

choose to forgive my father for leaving us, because it made me feel abandoned."
Tears will often come at this point, but this is not about trying to get somebody to
cry. It's making sure that it's as thorough as possible. One lady said, "I can't forgive
my mother. I hate her." Having recognized her real feelings of hatred, now for
probably the first time she could forgive — if she didn't admit that she hated her
mother, she wouldn't be able to forgive.

Pray as follows for each person you need to forgive: "Dear Heavenly Father, I
choose to forgive [name the person] for [what they did or failed to do], because it
made me feel [share the painful feelings, for example, rejected, dirty, worthless,
inferior]."

Take careful note of what is said after the statement "because it made me feel."
Usually the same word (for example, "abandoned," "stupid," "dirty") is repeated
several times. That may well reveal a stronghold that your past experiences have
led you to believe. You can tear down those strongholds by saying, for example: "I
renounce the lie that I am stupid. I announce the truth that I have the mind of
Christ" (1 Corinthians 2:16). "I renounce the lie that I am abandoned. I announce
the truth that God has promised never to leave me nor forsake me" (Hebrews
13:5). Session 8 of the *Freedom In Christ Course* teaches a specific strategy
("stronghhold-busting") that will enable you to do this effectively and the Freedom
In Christ app incorporates a "Stronghold-Buster Builder" that will be a great help.

7. Destroy the list
You are now free from those people and those events in the past.

8. Do not expect that forgiving others will result in changes in them
Forgiving others is primarily about you and your relationship with God. Pray for
those you have forgiven, that they may be blessed and that they too may find the
freedom of forgiveness (see Matthew 5:44; 2 Corinthians 2:7).

9. Try to understand the people you have forgiven
You may find it helpful to understand some of what the other person was going
through, but don't go so far as to rationalize away the sin — this is not about
saying "It didn't matter," because it did matter.

10. Expect positive results of forgiveness in you

Forgiveness is not about feeling good; it's about being free. However, good feelings will follow eventually. You will need to concentrate on renewing your mind so that negative ways of thinking are replaced by the truth.

11. Thank God for what you have learned and the maturity gained

You are now free to move on and grow as a Christian.

12. Accept your part of the blame for the offenses you suffered

Confess your part in any sin and know that you are forgiven. If you realize that someone has something against you, go to them and be reconciled. When you do that, be careful to simply confess your own wrongdoing rather than bringing up anything they did.

Dramatization
Matthew 18:21–35

Characters: **Peter, Jesus, Servant 1, Servant 2, Master**

Peter Lord, how many times shall I forgive my brother when he sins against me? Up to seven times?

Jesus I tell you, not seven times, but seventy-seven times.

Therefore, the kingdom of heaven is like a king who wanted to settle accounts with his servants. As he began the settlement, a man who owed him ten thousand talents was brought to him. Since he was not able to pay, the master ordered that he and his wife and his children and all that he had be sold to repay the debt.

The servant fell on his knees before him.

Servant 1 Be patient with me, and I will pay back everything.

Jesus The servant's master took pity on him, canceled the debt, and let him go. But when that servant went out, he found one of his fellow servants who owed him a hundred denarii. He grabbed him and began to choke him.

Servant 1	Pay back what you owe me!
Jesus	His fellow servant fell to his knees and begged him:
Servant 2	Be patient with me, and I will pay you back.
Jesus	But he refused. Instead, he went off and had the man thrown into prison until he could pay the debt. When the other servants saw what had happened, they were greatly distressed and went and told their master everything that had happened.
	Then the master called the servant in.
Master	You wicked servant, I canceled all that debt of yours because you begged me to. Shouldn't you have had mercy on your fellow servant just as I had on you?
Jesus	In anger his master turned him over to the jailers to be tortured, until he should pay back all he owed. This is how my heavenly Father will treat each of you unless you forgive your brother from your heart.

The Steps To Freedom In Christ

Resolve Personal And Spiritual Conflicts

This section is designed to give you some background information on The Steps To Freedom In Christ. *It is adapted with permission from* Break Free, Stay Free *by Steve Goss.*

The Steps To Freedom In Christ (The Steps) is a tool that Christians can use to take back any ground that has been given to the enemy by resolving personal and spiritual conflicts. It is a kind and gentle process contained in a separate booklet by Dr. Neil T. Anderson. You will be totally in control. I think you will love it!

I have been dismayed to hear that some churches (thankfully a small minority) loved the teaching sessions in the course but have not seen the need to take people through *The Steps To Freedom In Christ*. They have fallen for the Western worldview which predisposes us to think that good teaching alone is all that is needed for people to know the truth. Although some people are impacted and changed simply by hearing the truth of who they now are in Christ, the reality is that, if we leave in place the means the enemy has of interfering with our thinking, over time that gain is likely to be eroded. For others, although they may enjoy the sessions and appreciate the teaching, if they do not then go on to close doors open to the enemy to influence their minds, it is unlikely to have any lasting effect.

What are these personal and spiritual conflicts? As we have seen, Ephesians 4:26–27 says: "'In your anger do not sin': Do not let the sun go down while you are still angry, and do not give the devil a foothold."

If we allow anger to lead us into sin, we give the devil a "foothold" in our life. That word "foothold" is "topos" in Greek and literally means a "place." If Satan can lead us into sin, he can gain a "place," a point of influence in our lives. In terms of the battle for the mind, he gains some influence in our thinking. Those footholds seem to give him the ability to blind us to truth in much the same way as he blinds the minds of unbelievers (see 2 Corinthians 4:4).

That is the reason why we sometimes simply cannot grasp truth or hold on to it, why it seems to slip through our fingers.

I remember the first time this was brought home to me. I was taking someone through The Steps who looked like a normal, educated person with good eyesight. When I asked them to read the opening prayer, they stared at it for some time and declared that they could not read the words on the page. What was happening? Spiritual interference. There were so many points of influence for the enemy in that person's mind, that he was using them as best he could to prevent the process taking place. He was ultimately unsuccessful, of course, and at the end of the process, just to demonstrate the difference, I got them to read the prayer again, which, of course, was something they could do very easily once they had resolved the outstanding issues.

How are those issues resolved? Very simply and undramatically. The process is based on James 4:7: "Submit to God. Resist the devil and he will flee from you."

During *The Steps To Freedom In Christ*, you start by asking the Holy Spirit to show you any footholds that the enemy has in your life through past sin. As He shows you, you choose to repent and renounce and, because your power and authority in Christ is much greater than the enemy's, his right to influence you is taken away.

Having submitted to God, at the end of the process you command the enemy to leave your presence. Because you have dealt with the issues that the Holy Spirit has revealed to you, the enemy will have no option but to flee from you.

It is a kind and gentle process. You are in control and the outcome is in your hands. It's just between you and God. If you deal with everything the Holy Spirit shows you, at the end of the process you will be free in Christ. The Steps don't set you free, Jesus Christ does.

The Steps is simply a tool to help you cover the whole of your life history in one comprehensive session. It is something that I try to do once a year — it always amazes me how much rubbish I can accumulate in that time!

The *Freedom In Christ Course* lasts ten weeks. Do you know how long the early church spent discipling new converts? Three years! Most of that time was spent helping them deal with the kind of issues that are covered in The Steps. I would hate to think that people would treat this as some kind of one-off "program" that they can go through and say "Been there, done that." The real benefit comes when Christians get hold of the principles behind The Steps and take them deep into their lives so that taking hold of freedom and standing in it simply become part of how we live.

What Do The Steps Cover?

The Steps is an opportunity to put everything on the table before God at one time and ask Him to reveal anything that the enemy might be able to use to hold us back.

Let's run through the areas covered by The Steps to see what sort of sin can give ground to the enemy.

The Occult

The enemy may well have tempted you in the past to take part in an occult practice, often as "a bit of fun." However, in participating in that, no matter how it was dressed up, you were asking for guidance from the enemy. In the Old Testament, this was seen as such a serious issue that people who gave false guidance were to be stoned to death, and those who consulted them also faced stiff measures. There are similar warnings about false teachers and false prophets in the New Testament.

The issue at stake in The Steps is not your salvation but your fruitfulness as a Christian. Remember that you are in a battle against one who cannot do anything about the fact that you now belong to Christ but can attempt to make you a spiritual casualty, a Christian who does not bear fruit. Satan will use any means he can to hold you back. If he can find a way to influence your thinking, he will.

Some think that if something happened a long time ago, it cannot be of consequence now. That is not the case. Imagine the enemy as a crooked lawyer scrutinizing your past life with a magnifying glass looking for any loophole he can find to get the influence he is looking for. It's a bit like what sometimes happens in the political arena when someone puts themselves forward to run for a high profile post. Immediately their political enemies and some elements of the media start raking over their past to see what dirt they can find to hold them back. What you are doing in The Steps process is denying the enemy any possibility of finding a way to hold you back by resolving anything he may come up with.

In each of these areas, you start by asking the Holy Spirit to bring to your mind any unresolved sin that might allow the enemy to hold you back by influencing your thinking. In this first step, the Holy Spirit may bring to your mind an occasion when you participated in using the ouija board as a bit of a game at school. Is that really a problem? Well, if you asked the Holy Spirit to show you what the issues are and that came to your mind, it would be wise to assume that He has done just that and it is a problem. However, it really is straightforward to sort it out. You simply need to say something like, "I confess using the ouija board and I renounce it and take away any ground the enemy gained in my life." There is a prayer to use in The Steps book. Can just saying a few words really have any effect? If you mean them, they certainly can. Why? It's not the power of the words themselves so much as the power and authority of the one saying them — you are a child of God seated with Christ at the right hand of the Father! Your word carries weight.

This is similar to the way the early church acted. They would encourage people to say, "I renounce you Satan and all your works and all your ways." They would then specifically renounce every counterfeit religious experience they had, every false vow or pledge they made, and every false teacher or doctrine in which they believed.

We also need to look at our priorities and identify areas in our lives that have become more important to us than God. These are called 'idols'. Originally, the word referred to the false gods that the Old Testament Israelites were tempted to worship but our modern usage of the term is not so different.

Why were the Israelites tempted to worship Baal, a god of the Canaanites, for example? Because he was a fertility god and promised abundance in their crops as well as an opportunity for lust in fertility ceremonies. Is that so different to the idols we are tempted to worship such as material goods, money, and sex? The major difference, perhaps, is that it is easier for us to deceive ourselves that there isn't a problem.

Committing Ourselves To Truth

We are in a battle for truth. It is a battle between the father of lies (John 8:44) and the Spirit of Truth (John 16:13) and it takes place in our mind. We have already seen the importance of committing ourselves to truth. This needs to be an ongoing attitude.

Satan's strategies against us are essentially three-fold. He can tempt us, he can accuse us, and he can deceive us. Of the three, deception is by far the most powerful because if we are deceived, by definition we do not realize it.
It is not just Satan who sets out to deceive us. The world and the flesh have been doing that ever since we were born. We can also deceive ourselves.

The trouble is that deception, by definition, feels like truth.

In a way the whole steps process is about truth and lies. Most people come out of it with the ability to identify for the first time lies they have been believing and with a strategy to renew their minds.

Forgiving Others

Anyone you forgive, I also forgive. And what I have forgiven — if there was anything to forgive — I have forgiven in the sight of Christ for your sake, in order that Satan might not outwit us. For we are not unaware of his schemes.

(2 Corinthians 2:10–11)

If you want to see demonic activity in the Western Church, the place to look would be in division among Christians. In my experience nothing keeps you in bondage to the past more than an unwillingness to forgive. Nothing gives Satan greater opportunity to stop a church growing than roots of bitterness, unforgiveness, and backbiting.

We saw in Session 7 that in order to avoid the torment (or "torture") that comes from unforgiveness, Jesus says we need to forgive from the heart. What does it mean to forgive from the heart? It's simply being emotionally honest about what was done to us and just how much it hurt us and how wrong it was. It certainly doesn't mean saying a quick "I forgive so-and-so" and thinking it is dealt with. If we are truly going to forgive, we have to face the pain and the hate that we feel. We have to be honest with God.

In The Steps, we use this formula: "I choose to forgive [name the person] for [what they did or failed to do], because it made me feel [share the painful feelings, for example, rejected, dirty, worthless, inferior]." People are encouraged to be emotionally honest by telling God every hurt they remember and staying with it until they are sure it has all been put on the table. We have to let God lead us to the emotional core where the healing is going to take place.

I am not pretending that this is not painful or difficult. It is. However, this is not some kind of pointless exercise. It is done in order to resolve — completely resolve — this issue and get rid of the pain that we have been carrying around with us.

We cannot move on from the past until we forgive.

In no way is God asking you to sweep what was done under the carpet as if it did not matter. In fact quite the opposite. He promises that if you entrust the matter to Him, He will ensure that it is not swept under the carpet.

Look carefully at what He says:

> Do not take revenge, my friends, but leave room for God's wrath, for it is written: "It is mine to avenge; I will repay," says the Lord. (Romans 12:19)

When you forgive, although you are letting the person off your hook, you are not letting them off God's hook. When you choose to forgive, you are taking a step of faith to trust God to be the righteous judge who will make everything right in the end by demanding full payment for everything done against you. Nothing will be swept under the carpet. God really will demand justice for everything that has been done against you. Everyone who sinned against you will have to stand before God and explain it — either it will be paid for by the blood of Christ if the person is a Christian, or they will have to face the judgment of God if they are not. "I will repay" — God will settle every account some day.

You can hand all of that pain and those demands for justice and revenge over to God safe in the knowledge that He will repay. Justice will be done. In the meantime you can walk free of it.

Of course, that is not to say that the consequences of what was done can always be changed. When we forgive we have to come to terms with that and agree to live with the consequences of someone else's sin. That is not fair — but we have no choice. We will have to do it anyway. The only choice we have is whether we do it in freedom or bitterness.

Conversely some spend time worrying about whether what was done to them really was wrong. They wonder whether they misunderstood or think of some other reason why the person might have been justified in what they did. I always try to discourage people from thinking that way. In fact forgiveness is not primarily about objective right and wrong. It's about clearing rubbish out of your life and walking away from it. If you felt offended, you need to forgive whether or not the person was actually in the wrong or not.

When people go through The Steps we suggest that they consider whether they need to forgive God. Of course, from an objective point of view God has done nothing wrong — He is perfect. However, it's perfectly possible for us to feel that He has done wrong to us — perhaps we had been praying for someone to get better and they died; maybe we cannot understand why He let circumstances unfold as they did. If we have felt offended by God, even though we recognize intellectually that He has not acted wrongly, we need to release those feelings. If you feel uncomfortable saying "I forgive you God" you could say something like, "I release my feelings of hurt against you God."

We also suggest that they consider forgiving themselves. Many people so regret things they did in the past and bad choices they made that they will not let them go. They forgive other people but they will not forgive themselves. When they finally make that choice to forgive themselves, they are simply catching up with the reality that God has already completely forgiven them and made them new creations in Christ.

I received this letter from someone who was taken through *The Steps To Freedom In Christ*:

> We were led into a quiet time coming before God with a list of people we wanted to forgive. The Lord took me back to a time of great pain. Forty-one years ago I had a baby girl and was made to give her up for adoption. I had always blamed myself for not being strong enough to fight for her and keep her. As I was reliving this time in my mind the Lord asked me to forgive myself. I told Him I didn't know how to do this, it didn't seem enough to say the words.
>
> The Lord then gave me a picture of the baby lying in a crib beside me; she even had a little bonnet on. He asked me to lift her out and put her into His arms, saying she was His and He would care and look after her always and now I could forgive myself.
>
> I did as He asked and I know, without fully understanding, that a huge chain has been broken in the spiritual realms. God has given me freedom from the heavy guilt I had carried.

Rebellion

What would you do if you discovered that someone in your church was a practicing witch? That would be an interesting question for your leaders — I dare say that they would not ignore the matter.

What would you do if you discovered that someone in your church was rebellious, for example criticizing leaders, refusing to follow those whom God had placed in leadership roles? That is possibly an even more interesting question because you may well be able to think of people like that in your church already!

Here is an interesting verse in that context: "For rebellion is the same as witchcraft" (1 Samuel 15:23). In God's eyes, rebellion and witchcraft are pretty much the same thing, certainly in their degree of seriousness.

It's worth reading that verse through a few more times and pondering it. Because it does not seem to us as if witchcraft and rebellion are on a par. But God says they are.

The reason that rebellion may not seem that serious to us is because our view is easily colored by the world and, in our society, rebellion is the norm. There is a general lack of respect for those in government, for example, yet the Bible is clear that God established all governing authorities and requires us to be submissive (Romans 13:1–5; 1 Peter 2:13–17). Christians are often as guilty as the rest of society in harboring a rebellious spirit.

Of course, those that overstep the bounds of their authority do not have to be obeyed. We need submit only to authorities that act within their God-given boundaries. However, when they are doing that, our responsibility is to submit whether we agree with them or not.

When you choose to submit to a law that you regard as nonsensical (a speed limit perhaps) or a wife chooses to submit to a husband whom she knows is less than perfect, it is an act of faith in God. We are trusting God to protect us. He does not simply want us to submit outwardly but is looking for a sincere submission from the heart to those He has placed in authority over us.

When I think of submission I think back to when I was a child and I used to have mock wrestling fights with my father. When I had had enough I had to shout "I submit." In other words "I submit" was an admission of failure, of weakness. But for Christians submission is always a choice. God never forces us to do it. The ultimate example of a life of submission is Jesus himself:

> During the days of Jesus' life on earth, he offered up prayers and petitions with fervent cries and tears to the one who could save him from death, and he was heard because of his reverent submission. (Hebrews 5:7)

Choosing to submit to the authorities God has set up is a sign of great strength of character. Rebelling against God and the authorities He has set up is sin. It's a serious matter because it gives Satan an opportunity to attack. It is, therefore, in our own interests for our own spiritual protection, that we make the choice to live under the authority of God and those He has placed over us.

Pride

Here is a chilling verse from the Old Testament: "For though the LORD is high, he regards the lowly, but the haughty he knows from afar" (Psalm 138:6 ESV). God keeps His distance from the proud. If we are proud we will not hear His voice, we will not know His closeness. Pride is basically about thinking we can manage our own affairs without help from God or anyone else. If that is our attitude, God lets us get on with it. He knows that sooner or later we will discover the truth.

> Trust in the LORD with all your heart, and do not lean on your own understanding. In all your ways acknowledge him, and he will make straight your paths. Be not wise in your own eyes; fear the LORD, and turn away from evil. (Proverbs 3:5–7 ESV)

When we recognize the truth of how things are, we will know that we cannot accomplish anything of value on our own. We will turn to God in complete dependence. We will live in humility. We may have the impression that humility means being a doormat, allowing others to walk all over us. That is not a good definition. Paul said, "we put no confidence in the flesh" (Philippians 3:3) and that is a much better definition. We put no confidence in ourselves but choose instead to be "strong in the Lord, and in the strength of His might" (Ephesians 6:10). Being humble does not mean being a doormat. It means putting our confidence in God where it belongs.

Pride is the original sin of the devil. It sets one person or group against another — prejudice and bigotry are forms of pride. We hate to admit that there may be prejudice or bigotry in our hearts but it's another area where we need to come clean and be honest with God so that Satan does not gain any advantage in our lives.

Sin-Confess Cycles

All of us, including the Apostle Paul, know what it's like to be caught in a sin-confess cycle. Paul describes it like this:

> I do not understand what I do. For what I want to do I do not do, but what I hate I do. And if I do what I do not want to do, I agree that the law is good.
> (Romans 7:15–16)

You would be hard pressed to find a better description than that of what it feels like to be in bondage to sin. Here is someone who knows what is right and wants to do what is right but for some reason just can't. Paul, however, learned to resolve them. He says that what he calls "the law of sin and of death" still pulls us toward sin every day but we have access to a greater law, a more powerful law, "the law of the Spirit of life in Christ Jesus." Normally we cannot fly because the law of gravity prevents us. However, when we get into a plane, we find we can fly. The law of gravity has not been suspended but we overcome it by a greater law, that of aerodynamics and the forward thrust of the engine. Although the law of sin and death is still working, we have access to a greater law and can fly above sin and death by the power of the Spirit of life.

Although it feels as if there is nothing we can do to get out of the predicament, the truth is that we do not have to let the flesh rule. If we have allowed sin to reign in our bodies, we can put a stop to it. Addictions are particularly deep-rooted sin-confess cycles. Like other strongholds, they usually start as coping mechanisms. Very often they are used to cope with emotional pain. Like any other sin, however, we can expect to see them completely resolved in Christ.

Sometimes it is enough for an addict to understand who they are in Christ. Once you realize that you are simply a product of Christ's work on the cross and not a product of the past, much of the pain of past experiences is taken away. Usually, however, it is necessary to do more work but the approach is the same as for other sin-confess cycles.

I have seen Christians kick addictions to binge-eating, anorexia, drugs, alcohol, and other things through understanding their identity in Christ, then submitting to God and resisting the devil. I have every admiration for Alcoholics Anonymous and the great work they do. However, I have come to realize that if it's a Christian who has the alcohol issue, although they very much do need to own up to the problem, it is not necessarily helpful for them to identify themselves as "an alcoholic" as if that were part of their identity. The truth is that they are not an alcoholic — their fundamental identity is that of a child of God. A correct assessment would be to say that they are a child of God with an alcohol problem. That problem can be fully resolved in Christ. They do not have to drink. Instead they can be filled with the Spirit. The alcohol problem is not part of who they are. In fact it goes right against who they are — in drinking to excess they are acting completely out of character.

Here is the story of a Christian who had been struggling with smoking:

I had had numerous failed attempts at stopping smoking since I'd restarted again but I couldn't even last 24 hours. I was extremely embarrassed that I smoked, especially as I was leading so many Freedom Appointments and yet wasn't walking in complete freedom myself.

Anyway, last May I sat down with God. I had sussed out that when I thought about certain people or events, or anything sometimes, I would get what felt like a physical sensation inside which was extremely unpleasant, a bit like dread and fear and loss, and which smoking got rid of instantly.

I've been taught well by Freedom In Christ and know that what I'm thinking about will have a direct impact on my feelings so I knew it was to do with my thoughts and the battle for my mind. So I asked God about His advice to take every thought captive in obedience to Jesus. The way I'm wired, to be able to do something I need to be able to understand what He means. So I asked Him what He meant.

He said, "If you were in the army and you caught an enemy, you wouldn't take him back to your quarters and sit him in the corner of your room and have a chat with him. No, what you'd do, without hesitation, would be to take that enemy to the place your Commanding Officer had designated for him. Well, you're in My army and your Commanding Officer is Jesus, so all that is required of you is for you to obediently take every captured thought to Jesus and He'll deal with them." And it was that simple. I soon became very aware of what was going on in my mind whereas before I let it wander around all over the place. I put a kind of mental butterfly net in there and could almost see myself catching thoughts and then I'd say something like, "Jesus, I've caught these thoughts and I'm giving them to You obediently," and within seconds the feelings that had risen up in me were replaced with peace and the desire to grab a cigarette was gone. Often when the battle was really intense, I didn't feel like I was doing much else than catch thoughts but as I did my part, God did the miracle bit. I've no idea how He did the miracle bit but together we did it, and I've not smoked for over 13 months. Praise Him!

Sexual Sin

Flee from sexual immorality. All other sins a man commits are outside his body, but he who sins sexually sins against his own body. Do you not know that your body is a temple of the Holy Spirit, who is in you, whom you have received from God? You are not your own; you were bought at a price. Therefore honor God with your body.

(1 Corinthians 6:13–20).

We have more than just a spiritual union with God. Although they are temporary, our physical bodies are spiritually significant. In fact, our bodies are "members of Christ himself" and "a temple of the Holy Spirit." Sexual sin defiles God's temple.

What happens when a child of God (united with the Lord and one spirit with Him) also unites with a prostitute and becomes one with her in body? They become "one flesh" — they are bonded together. This bonding mechanism is a gift from God created specifically for a marriage relationship whereby a man and woman commit themselves to each other before Him. Using it outside that relationship, either with a prostitute as in Paul's example or with anyone else, has consequences — a spiritual bonding takes place.

What does that mean in practice? As you would expect, like any other sin, sexual sin gives the enemy a foothold that he can use to gain influence in our minds. However, it seems to do more than that. It can serve to draw us back to the same person or to the same sin again and again.

How many times have you come across someone who is clearly unhappy in a sexual relationship outside marriage and wants to break it off but somehow never can, or, even if they do, end up going back to a partner who they know is going to mistreat them in some way? They are bonded, they are one flesh. There would still be a hold and a pull back even if they did manage to break the relationship.

We can, however, take back ground that we have given to the enemy. Even when we have defiled God's temple, in His grace He can make us completely pure again. We need to close the doors we have opened to the enemy and break any sinful bonds that we have formed. We can then present our bodies back to God as living sacrifices, committing, as far as sexual activity is concerned, to reserve them exclusively for marriage.

If you are not married, keep your body as a gift for your future spouse should God provide one for you. You are too special to allow it to be defiled.

The wonderful thing is that no matter how many past sexual experiences you may have had or what they were, Christ resolves them completely. You are no longer dirty or unacceptable.

Inherited Consequences Of Sin

The Bible is clear that the consequences of sin (not the guilt for them) pass down generations. In other words, we can inherit vulnerability to a particular sin from our parents and more distant ancestors in much the same way that we have all inherited the consequences of Adam's sin.

This is another area which the Western worldview predisposes us to overlook because it is not within our experience. The result of that is that it is all too easy to leave these spiritual vulnerabilities in place when they could be dealt with straightforwardly.

None of us has any difficulty recognizing that we have a genetic inheritance from our ancestors. Our genes determine our physical characteristics and, according to scientists, can determine our vulnerability to certain character traits. It is claimed, for example, that certain gene combinations make it more likely that someone will become an alcoholic. However, nobody claims that they make this inevitable. Personal choice is ultimately more important than the genes.

We also recognize that the environment we were brought up in has a significant effect on our character and values. As Jesus said, "A student is not above his teacher, but everyone who is fully trained will be like his teacher" (Luke 6:40). That too is something that we inherit from past generations and something that we can choose to perpetuate or not.

As in many areas of life, the same principles that apply in the physical realm apply in the spiritual realm too. There are many places in the Old Testament that explicitly outline the principle of consequences of sin passing down generations, the most significant being in the Ten Commandments themselves:

> You shall not make for yourself an idol in the form of anything in heaven above or on the earth beneath or in the waters below. You shall not bow down to them or worship them; for I, the Lord your God, am a jealous God, punishing the children for the sin of the fathers to the third and fourth generation of those who hate me, but showing love to a thousand generations of those who love me and keep my commandments. (Exodus 20:4–6)

God blesses obedience to a thousand generations but, in His grace, allows the effects of sin to pass down only three or four generations. Yet it is clear that they do pass down. Paul explains that positive spiritual blessings pass down from Christian parents to children (1 Corinthians 7:14–15). This is an example of the same principle operating but with a good spiritual heritage rather than a bad one.

But, some may say, didn't Jesus deal with our sin at the cross? Yes. He dealt with our guilt. But we never were guilty for the sins of our ancestors — each person is responsible for their own sin. But that sin may cause consequences for others in much the same way that someone who was physically harmed by a mugger may walk with a limp — they were not guilty for that sin but they suffer the consequences.

Each one of us, then, is born with genetic, environmental, and spiritual dispositions. These can be good or bad. We need actively to take a stand against the bad elements of our inheritance otherwise we simply leave them in place and they remain effective. In particular, we need to take steps to deal with any footholds of the enemy that we inherited as a result of past sin in order to make sure the enemy cannot hold us back.

Given that in Christ we have much more spiritual power and authority than the enemy does, this is not a difficult issue. We simply ask the Holy Spirit to make us aware of what the issues are and then actively renounce them.

It is simple and straightforward but for some people it makes an enormous difference. A good friend of mine began experiencing headaches and severe spiritual "interference" during The Steps process. He sensed that the Holy Spirit was saying that there was Freemasonry (which is steeped in the occult) in his family background. As soon as he renounced it, the interference and headaches stopped.

I can think too of a Christian couple who had some issues in their marriage. He had already been married twice before and, as he looked back at his family line, he realized that on both sides of his family as far back down the generations as he could remember there was divorce. As he came to renounce divorce, he experienced real spiritual opposition and struggled even to say the word. However, as soon as he had, the opposition disappeared. He realized that he had entered his present marriage with something of a caveat — "well, if it doesn't work, we can always get divorced." Afterward, he and his wife renewed their wedding vows and have gone on to maintain a firm emphasis on "till death us do part" in their now strong marriage.

This is one area that most of us simply have never had any teaching on. The result is that we leave the enemy some ability to hold us back when we don't have to. So, you have an exciting opportunity to deal with any area in your life where the enemy may be holding you back. Remember, the effects of that will show up in our mind and, because he is the master of deception, we probably do not even recognize them. It is only when we humbly come to God and ask Him to reveal to us what the problems are, that many of them become apparent for the first time.

The good news is that *The Steps To Freedom In Christ* process is a kind, gentle, and usually matter-of-fact process that helps us to exercise the amazing spiritual authority we now have and deal with them.

There is nothing too big for you and God!

Renewing The Mind

WHAT'S IT ABOUT?

OBJECTIVE: To understand that taking hold of — and living in — your freedom in Christ is not a one-off experience but needs to become a way of life, and to provide you with a strategy to continually renew your mind.

FOCUS VERSE: Do not conform to the pattern of this world, but be transformed by the renewing of your mind. Then you will be able to test and approve what God's will is — his good, pleasing and perfect will. (Romans 12:2)

FOCUS TRUTH: All of us have mental strongholds, ways of thinking that are not in line with God's truth. Our success in continuing to walk in freedom and grow in maturity depends on the extent to which we continue to renew our minds and train ourselves to distinguish good from evil.

> The third book in the FREEDOM IN CHRIST DISCIPLESHIP SERIES, *Break Free, Stay Free*, corresponds to Part C of the course. The accompanying material for this session is on pages 99–110.

WELCOME

How did you find *The Steps To Freedom In Christ* process?

WORSHIP

He has set me free! Galatians 5:1, Psalm 119:45.

WORD

Ongoing Transformation

You became a brand new creation when you first turned to Jesus. But now the stage is set for you to be transformed further. When that word is used in the Bible it refers to the process through which a caterpillar becomes a beautiful butterfly. It doesn't mean changed just a little bit — it means a really dramatic change. How do you think that ongoing transformation happens? What do you need to do to experience it?

> Do not conform to the pattern of this world, but be transformed by the renewing of your mind. (Romans 12:2a)

Remember, the battle is for our minds. Our minds have been conditioned by the world, influenced by Satan the puppet master behind it. So we've developed a whole host of default beliefs and thought patterns that don't match up with God's Word. In other words, they are not actually true.

For much of our lives, our belief system has been shaped by our enemies. In other words, we've absorbed a whole load of lies and half-truths that really affect us. When we became Christians no one pressed a delete button in our minds. We still have the same old default programming, those same old thought patterns, or what the Bible calls "the flesh."

Taking hold of our freedom is essential, but is not enough. Now, we need to change that default thinking if we want to grow as disciples. We need to replace it with what is actually true. And the key to that is renewing our minds.

Strongholds

For though we live in the world we do not wage war as the world does. The weapons we fight with are not the weapons of the world. On the contrary, they have divine power to demolish strongholds. We demolish arguments and every pretension that sets itself up against the knowledge of God, and we take every thought captive to make it obedient to Christ. (2 Corinthians 10:3–5)

Paul is clearly talking of something in the area of our thinking. He mentions **arguments** and every **pretension** that sets itself up against the true **knowledge** of God. He talks about taking every **thought** captive to make it obedient to Christ. The literal meaning of the word "stronghold" is a fortress, a strong defensive

building. In this context a stronghold is a faulty belief that has been reinforced many times over a long period. It prevents you knowing God and His ways. It's sitting there in your mind apparently strong and impenetrable — like a thick castle wall.

Perhaps it started out right back in childhood when a little thought was planted in your mind by something that happened to you — maybe you were bullied, or worse — or someone said something negative about you: "You're useless," "You're a failure," "You're ugly," "It's all your fault."

Maybe the enemy lined up someone else at a different time who said or did the same thing. Since he knows your particular vulnerabilities, he ruthlessly tries to exploit them by lining up people or circumstances one after the other to give you the same wrong message.

The world then adds insult to injury with its constant bombardment of lies about what it means to be successful or happy or loved.

As it gets stronger and stronger, it becomes part of our default thinking and works itself out in our behavior. Then, whenever someone suggests we could go for a particular job or lead a small group at church, a tape plays in our mind, "I couldn't do that. I'm useless at that." We've believed it for so long it becomes part of our lives and we can't imagine it ever being any different.

A good definition of a stronghold is **a belief or habitual pattern of thinking that is not consistent with what God tells us is true**.

Feelings of inferiority, insecurity, and inadequacy are all strongholds. Because no child of God is inferior, insecure, or inadequate.

Is any child of God dirty or ugly? Absolutely not. It isn't true. It just **feels** true. It's a lie that's been reinforced so many times that it literally has a strong hold on you and causes you to think and act in ways that contradict God's Word.

Strongholds can have two faces: when we know what we should do but don't seem able to do it; and when know we shouldn't do something but don't seem able to stop.

PAUSE FOR THOUGHT 1

"My entire personality has been formed around the wrong information." What do you think about the idea that for much of our lives, our belief system and how we think have been influenced and shaped by many lies and half-truths said over us?

"No child of God is inferior or inadequate." Discuss.

What practical ways can we consider to make us more aware of strongholds, and how they affect our lives?

How Strongholds Are Established

Our Environment

We have already seen how we learn values and beliefs from the world we live in. It also can work at the micro-level in our home, school, or work environment.

We call them "strongholds" but psychologists might call them "defense mechanisms." They are ways of thinking and acting that have become deeply ingrained in the mind.

Traumatic Experiences

It doesn't necessarily take something to be repeated over a long period of time to set up a stronghold. A one-time powerful traumatic experience can do it because of its intensity: a divorce, a rape, or a death in the home. For example, if you were abused, you may come to see yourself as a victim: helpless; never able to stand up for yourself. At one time that may have been true but that's not true any more if you are a child of God.

It's not the traumatic experience itself that produces the stronghold. It's the lie we believe as a result of that traumatic experience.

Whatever has happened to you in the past, you can go back to that traumatic event and process it again from the position of who you are now: a holy child of God. No Christian, no matter how bad their past experiences, has to remain a victim. God doesn't change our past, He sets us free from it!

Giving In To Temptation

Tempting thoughts that are not dealt with will immediately lead on to actions. Repeating the action will lead to a habit. Exercising the habit long enough will produce a stronghold.

Satan is actively trying to tempt you into the same sin time and time again because he wants to set up strongholds in your life so that he can keep you going round in circles feeling hopeless.

The Bible is clear that there is a way out of every temptation. There is a short extra teaching film on the app that looks at this in more detail.

If you drive a truck across a muddy field, it will create some ruts (grooves) in the field. If you drive the same way every day over a period of time, the ruts will get deeper and deeper and more noticeable. Eventually they will be so well established that you could let go of the steering wheel and the truck would drive itself. That's fine as long as the ruts are going in the right direction. Strongholds are like ruts that are heading in the wrong direction. If you don't intentionally change the direction, you are taking your hands off the steering wheel of your life and you are likely to end up somewhere you don't want to go.

The problem with strongholds is that they lead us to act on lies — false information — and cause our feelings to be out of line with reality. You may feel rejection when you are not actually being rejected. You may feel helpless to change when you are not helpless at all, for example you may feel that you will never get out of a particular sin when in fact you have everything you need to walk away from it.

Freedom And Maturity Are Not The Same

The moment you turn to Jesus you are not expected to be instantly mature. When babies are born they drink milk for a while before they move on to solid food. But if babies keep acting like babies as they get older, they become less attractive!

Any Christian can become an old Christian — all it takes is time! Any Christian can become a mature Christian — but many don't because they don't know how to deal with their strongholds.

PAUSE FOR THOUGHT 2

Spend some time discussing the ways that strongholds are established. In what ways can you identify with the story of the alcoholic father and his three sons? Can you see any strongholds that have been established in your own life?

Look at this list of common lies that people come to believe about themselves: unloved, rejected, inadequate, hopeless, stupid. For each one, find a Bible verse to show that it cannot be true of any Christian.

"No Christian, no matter how bad their past experiences, has to remain a victim. God doesn't change our past, He sets us free from it!" Discuss.

Demolishing Strongholds

Close Doors Open To The Enemy

In *The Steps To Freedom In Christ* you have taken away the footholds the enemy had in your life and that's a key reason that you can now demolish strongholds, even those that you may have tried time and again to deal with in the past but failed.

Take Personal Responsibility For The Whole Of Your Life

This is not about asking God or someone else to do something in order for us to get free or grow. You already have everything you need to live a godly life (2 Peter 1:3).

In the way God has set things up, some things are His responsibility and some things are our responsibility. If we don't do the things that He has given us to do, they simply won't get done.

No one else can forgive for you. And no one else can choose to believe the truth for you.

On the app you'll find a very useful extra teaching film about working out who is responsible for what.

Take Every Thought Captive (2 Corinthians 10:5)

You can think of your mind as being like an airport and you are the air traffic controller. A lot of thoughts ask for permission to land. But you have complete control over which will land and which will be turned away.

We are in a battle between truth and lies. Every stronghold is an entrenched lie. The key to demolishing it is to uncover the lie behind it and then replace the lie with the truth.

Be Transformed Through The Renewing Of Your Mind

You can use a tool that we call "stronghold-busting" to renew your mind. It's outlined on the opposite page and there is a Stronghold-Buster Builder in the app to help you.

Don't treat this stronghold-busting as some kind of magic however! It's not the speaking out that will change you, and there's not some special formula that works for everyone. Don't get all religious either — if you miss a day or two, God still loves you! Just pick it up the next day and carry on.

Do persevere until you have completed a total of 40 days. In fact you may wish to go on longer and you will almost certainly want to come back and do it again at some point in the future.

It may sound easy but it's not — because the lie feels true to you. It's like watching a concrete wall being demolished. It withstands 10, then 15, then 30, then 35 blows with no visible sign of being weakened. That's how it can feel as you work through a stronghold-buster day after day. However, each day you renounce the lie and commit yourself to truth is making a difference. Eventually the wall will collapse.

Stronghold-Busting

Work out the lie you have been believing
This is any way you have learned to think that is not in line with what God says in the Bible. Ignore what you feel because, by definition, the lie will feel true.

Say what effect believing the lie has had in your life
Imagine how different your life would be if you did not believe this. What would you be able to do that you currently don't do?

Find as many Bible verses as you can that say what is actually true and write them down
If there are a lot of verses, pick the top seven or eight.

Write a declaration
Base it on this formula: "I renounce the lie that . . . , I announce the truth that . . ."

If you prefer, you could use alternative language such as "I reject the lie that . . . , I embrace the truth that . . ." or "I say no to the lie that . . . , I say yes to the truth that . . ."

Read the Bible verses and say the declaration out loud every day for 40 days
Remember that for a long time, the verses and the declaration will not **feel** true.

Remind yourself that God is the Truth and that if He has said it, it really is true. And it's not just true for other people, it's true for you!

You can use the app to remind you to make your declaration.

Commit For The Long Term

Forgetting what is behind and straining toward what is ahead, I press on toward the goal to win the prize for which God has called me heavenward in Christ Jesus. All of us who are mature should take such a view of things. (Philippians 3:13b–15a)

If we feel we have to do everything at once we are likely to start but not finish, to burn out and conclude that we have failed. If, however, we set out a long term plan, we can deal with one area at a time and make sure that we really have changed our thinking before moving on to the next area. In a year we could deal with eight or nine areas — and that would make a tremendous difference.

Every single one of us can know that absolutely nothing and no one can stop us becoming the people God wants us to be as long as we play our part and use the weapons He has already put into our hands.

REFLECTION

Have you become aware of lies that you are prone to believe? What is the most significant one?

Use this time to create — or start to create — your very own stronghold-buster so that you can go on to demolish it. Use the guidelines on page 155 of your Participant's Guide and take note of the sample stronghold-busters on pages 159–161. There is space to create your own stronghold-busters on pages 162–167. You can also use the app.

WITNESS

Write down the two most important things you have learned in this course so far. How do you think you could explain them to a not-yet Christian?

IN THE COMING WEEK

Complete your stronghold-buster for the most significant lie you have uncovered and start going through it. You could use the Stronghold-Buster Builder on the app to create it and to alert you every day to go through it.

Stronghold-Buster Example 1
Taking Comfort In Food Rather Than God

The lie: that overeating brings lasting comfort.

Effects in my life: harmful to health; getting overweight; giving the enemy a foothold; stopping my growth to maturity.

Proverbs 25:28: Like a city whose walls are broken through is a person who lacks self-control.

Galatians 5:16: So I say, live by the Spirit, and you will not gratify the desires of the flesh.

Galatians 5:22–24: But the fruit of the Spirit is love, joy, peace, patience, kindness, goodness, faithfulness, gentleness and self-control. Against such things there is no law. Those who belong to Christ Jesus have crucified the flesh with its passions and desires.

2 Corinthians 1:3–4: Praise be to the God and Father of our Lord Jesus Christ, the Father of compassion and the God of all comfort, who comforts us in all our troubles, so that we can comfort those in any trouble with the comfort we ourselves have received from God.

Psalm 63:4–5: I will praise you as long as I live, and in your name I will lift up my hands. My soul will be satisfied as with the richest of foods; with singing lips my mouth will praise you.

Psalm 119:76: May your unfailing love be my comfort.

God, I renounce the lie that overeating brings lasting comfort. I announce the truth that You are the God of all comfort and that Your unfailing love is my only legitimate and real comfort. I affirm that I now live by the Spirit and do not have to gratify the desires of the flesh. Whenever I feel in need of comfort, instead of turning to foods I choose to praise You and be satisfied as with the richest of foods. Fill me afresh with Your Holy Spirit and live through me as I grow in self-control. Amen.

Tick off the days:

1	2	3	4	5	6	7	8	9
10	11	12	13	14	15	16	17	18
19	20	21	22	23	24	25	26	27
28	29	30	31	32	33	34	35	36
37	38	39	40					

Stronghold-Buster Example 2
Always Feeling Alone

The lie: that I am abandoned and forgotten.

Effects in my life: withdrawing from others; thinking people don't like me; seeming aloof; frightened.

Deuteronomy 31:6: Be strong and courageous. Do not be afraid or terrified because of them, for the LORD your God goes with you; he will never leave you nor forsake you.

Isaiah 46:4: Even to your old age and gray hairs I am he, I am he who will sustain you. I have made you and I will carry you; I will sustain you and I will rescue you.

Jeremiah 29:11: "For I know the plans I have for you," declares the LORD, "plans to prosper you and not to harm you, plans to give you hope and a future."

Romans 8:38–39: For I am convinced that neither death nor life, neither angels nor demons, neither the present nor the future, nor any powers, neither height nor depth, nor anything else in all creation, will be able to separate us from the love of God that is in Christ Jesus our Lord.

Dear Heavenly Father,
I say no to the lie that I am abandoned and forgotten and will be left on my own.
I say yes to the truth that You love me, that You have plans to give me a hope and
a future and that absolutely nothing can separate me from Your love.
In Jesus' name. Amen.

Tick off the days:

1	2	3	4	5	6	7	8	9
10	11	12	13	14	15	16	17	18
19	20	21	22	23	24	25	26	27
28	29	30	31	32	33	34	35	36
37	38	39	40					

Stronghold-Buster Example 3
Feeling Irresistibly Drawn To Porn

The lie: that I cannot resist the temptation to look at porn.
Effects in my life: deep sense of shame; warped sexual feelings; unable to relate to other people as God intended; harmful to my marriage.

Romans 6:11–14: In the same way, count yourselves dead to sin but alive to God in Christ Jesus. Therefore do not let sin reign in your mortal body so that you obey its evil desires. Do not offer any part of yourself to sin as an instrument of wickedness, but rather offer yourselves to God as those who have been brought from death to life; and offer every part of yourself to him as an instrument of righteousness. For sin shall no longer be your master, because you are not under the law, but under grace.

1 Corinthians 6:19: Do you not know that your body is a temple of the Holy Spirit?

1 Corinthians 10:13: No temptation has overtaken you except what is common to mankind. And God is faithful; he will not let you be tempted beyond what you can bear. But when you are tempted, he will also provide a way out so that you can endure it.

Galatians 5:16: So I say, live by the Spirit, and you will not gratify the desires of the flesh.

Galatians 5:22–23a: But the fruit of the Spirit is love, joy, peace, patience, kindness, goodness, faithfulness, gentleness and self-control.

I reject the lie that I cannot resist the temptation to look at porn. I embrace the truth that God will always provide a way out when I am tempted and I will choose to take it. I announce the truth that if I live by the Spirit — and I choose to do that — I will not gratify the desires of the flesh and the fruit of the Spirit, including self-control, will grow in me. I count myself dead to sin and refuse to let sin reign in my body or be my master. Today and every day I give my body to God as a temple of the Holy Spirit to be used only for what honors Him. I declare that the power of sin is broken in me. I choose to submit completely to God and resist the devil who must flee from me now.

Tick off the days:

1	2	3	4	5	6	7	8	9
10	11	12	13	14	15	16	17	18
19	20	21	22	23	24	25	26	27
28	29	30	31	32	33	34	35	36
37	38	39	40					

My Stronghold-Buster 1

1. What lie do you want to tackle?

2. What effect does this faulty belief have on your life? How different would your life be if you replaced it with what is actually true?

3. List as many Bible verses as you can that state what God says is actually true then pick the top seven or eight:

4. Write a prayer/declaration:

I renounce the lie that

I announce the truth that

5. Read the Bible verses and say the prayer/declaration out loud every day for forty days. You can set the Freedom In Christ app to remind you each day.

Mark off the days below:

1	2	3	4	5	6	7	8	9
10	11	12	13	14	15	16	17	18
19	20	21	22	23	24	25	26	27
28	29	30	31	32	33	34	35	36
37	38	39	40					

My Stronghold-Buster 2

1.   What lie do you want to tackle?

2.   What effect does this faulty belief have on your life? How different would your life be if you replaced it with what is actually true?

3.   List as many Bible verses as you can that state what God says is actually true then pick the top seven or eight:

4. Write a prayer/declaration:

I renounce the lie that

I announce the truth that

5. Read the Bible verses and say the prayer/declaration out loud every day for forty days. You can set the Freedom In Christ app to remind you each day.

Mark off the days below:

1	2	3	4	5	6	7	8	9
10	11	12	13	14	15	16	17	18
19	20	21	22	23	24	25	26	27
28	29	30	31	32	33	34	35	36
37	38	39	40					

My Stronghold-Buster 3

1. What lie do you want to tackle?

2. What effect does this faulty belief have on your life? How different would your life be if you replaced it with what is actually true?

3. List as many Bible verses as you can that state what God says is actually true then pick the top seven or eight:

4. Write a prayer/declaration:

I renounce the lie that

I announce the truth that

5. Read the Bible verses and say the prayer/declaration out loud every day for forty days. You can set the Freedom In Christ app to remind you each day.

Mark off the days below:

1	2	3	4	5	6	7	8	9
10	11	12	13	14	15	16	17	18
19	20	21	22	23	24	25	26	27
28	29	30	31	32	33	34	35	36
37	38	39	40					

GROWING AS DISCIPLES

Having taken hold of our freedom in Christ, we now need to concentrate on growing to maturity. In this final section we will learn the critical importance of relating well to others, and how to ensure that we stay on the path of becoming more and more like Jesus.

Relating To Others

WHAT'S IT ABOUT?

OBJECTIVE: To understand our roles and responsibilities in relationships so that we can grow together in Christ and express true unity.

FOCUS VERSE: Jesus replied: "'Love the Lord your God with all your heart and with all your soul and with all your mind.' This is the first and greatest commandment. And the second is like it: 'Love your neighbor as yourself.' All the Law and the Prophets hang on these two commandments." (Matthew 22:37–40)

FOCUS TRUTH: As disciples of Christ we will want to be part of the answer to Jesus' prayer that we will be one. In learning to relate well to others, we need to assume responsibility for our own character and seek to meet the needs of others, rather than the other way round.

> You'll find more information on this final section of the course in the fourth book in the FREEDOM IN CHRIST DISCIPLESHIP SERIES, *The You God Planned*. See pages 77–92 for the material that relates specifically to this session.

WELCOME

Have you ever done something that offended someone else without realizing at the time that you had caused offense? Tell the story briefly.

WORSHIP

Praising God for those people He has brought into our lives. 1 John 3:16.

WORD

The Importance Of Unity

Jesus' Prayer For You

There is an occasion where Jesus prayed a prayer specifically for you. It comes shortly before He went to the cross and He's been praying for His disciples. This is what He says next:

"My prayer is not for them alone. I pray also for those who will believe in me through their message, that all of them may be one, Father, just as you are in me and I am in you. May they also be in us so that the world may believe that you have sent me." (John 17:20–21)

Free Will Gives Us Responsibility

This is not a prayer that God can actually answer. In His wisdom and humility God has given every human being personal responsibility for the choices we make.

He could have chosen to make us like robots so that if we wanted to criticize what someone else believes or wanted to lash out against them in anger, we'd find that we just couldn't do it — the words wouldn't come out. But He hasn't done that. He gave us free will. We are completely free to choose not to be one and God does not overrule despite Jesus' prayer.

So why does Jesus pray this prayer at all? Surely He is sending a message to us that unity is the most important thing for us to focus on.

Isn't preaching the Gospel more important than unity? Look at why He says He wants us to be one: "So that the world may believe that you have sent me." It seems that our unity will in fact lead directly to people being saved.

Changing The "Spiritual Atmosphere"

Why don't more people in your community respond to the Gospel? You may point out that techniques could be improved, that there aren't enough workers going into the harvest, or any number of other perfectly valid reasons. But our Western worldview tends to predispose us to overlook verses like 2 Corinthians 4:4:

> The god of this age has blinded the minds of unbelievers, so that they cannot see the light of the gospel that displays the glory of Christ, who is the image of God.

Compare that with Psalm 133 which starts by saying: "How good and pleasant it is when God's people live together in unity!" and concludes, "For there the Lord bestows his blessing, even life forevermore."

There is more going on than each individual's response to God. Every community is a potential harvest field but the seeds need light in order to grow. Satan wants to keep it in darkness but as the Church repents of its sin and works as the one body that it actually is, he can't do that and light comes in. The result is that more people will respond to the Gospel as the workers go out into the harvest field. It seems that repentance and unity can effect a positive change in what you might call "the spiritual atmosphere."

Illustration 1

Imagine a scene of a huge field of wheat ready to harvested. In one corner is a man cutting the wheat with a scythe, a small hand-held blade. He works and works but makes hardly any impression. It's obvious that he can only harvest a tiny part of the potential of that field. Yet back in the farmyard is a brand new combine harvester, the sort that could do the whole job in a couple of hours. But it can't be used because it's in pieces — all the parts are scattered across the farmyard.

If God's people are not genuinely united we will only ever reach a tiny part of the harvest.

Illustration 2

Imagine a huge gushing waterfall coming over a cliff. Yet the riverbed at the bottom is bone dry and, because no water is flowing out, the land at the bottom is a desert where nothing is growing. The reason there is no water is because there are deep fissures in the river bed and the water is simply disappearing down the cracks. If the cracks could be filled in, then the water would run down the riverbed and irrigate the land. And plants would begin to grow.

Even though God is pouring out His Spirit upon us, if there are cracks in our unity, the effects will be nowhere near as great as they could be.

> Make every effort to keep the unity of the Spirit through the bond of peace. There is one body and one Spirit, just as you were called to one hope when you were called; one Lord, one faith, one baptism; one God and Father of all, who is over all and through all and in all. (Ephesians 4:3–6)

Understanding How God Comes To Us

"We love because he first loved us" (1 John 4:19). We give freely because we have received freely (Matthew 10:8). We are merciful because he has been merciful to us (Luke 6:36), and we forgive in the same way that Jesus has forgiven us (Ephesians 4:32).

If we truly understand how God comes to us and we go to others in the same way, we won't go far wrong.

Being Aware Of Our Own Weaknesses

When Isaiah was praying in the temple He saw a vision of God Himself "seated on a throne, high and exalted" (Isaiah 6:1). If that happened to you, would you immediately start thinking of the shortcomings of other people? No, you'd do what Isaiah did and cry out, "Woe to me! I am ruined! . . . For I am a man of unclean lips" (Isaiah 6:5).

In Luke 5:4 Peter has been fishing all night without success and Jesus says to him, "Put out into deep water, and let down the nets for a catch." Peter obeys, goes back to the lake and starts pulling in fish after fish. He must have suddenly realized just who was in the boat with him. How did he respond? "I am a sinful man" (verse 8).

When we see God for who He is, we don't become aware of the sin of others, but of our own sin. But when we are lukewarm in our relationship with God, we tend to overlook our own sin and see the sin of others and want to point it out to them.

PAUSE FOR THOUGHT 1

2 Corinthians 4:4 says that one reason people do not respond to the Gospel is that Satan has blinded their minds, and Psalm 133 says that where there is unity, God brings blessing. How do these verses help you understand why Jesus prayed that we would be one?

"If God's people are not genuinely united we will only ever reach a tiny part of the harvest." What are your thoughts on this statement?

"When we are lukewarm in our relationship with God, we tend to overlook our own sin and see the sin of others." Discuss this idea.

We Are Responsible For Our Own Character And Others' Needs

Who are you to judge someone else's servant? To their own master, servants stand or fall. And they will stand, for the Lord is able to make them stand. (Romans 14:4)

It's not for us to judge someone else's **character** because it's none of our business. A growing disciple is someone who is becoming more and more like Jesus in character — no one else can do that for us and we can't do it for someone else.

Do nothing out of selfish ambition or vain conceit. Rather, in humility value others above yourselves, not looking to your own interests but each of you to the interests of the others. In your relationships with one another, have the same mindset as Christ Jesus. (Philippians 2:3–5)

Not only do I have no right to expect my needs to be met by others, I have a responsibility to meet their needs!

Our responsibilities can be summed up as: developing our own character and meeting the needs of others.

Focus On Responsibilities Rather Than Rights

In every relationship we have rights and we also have responsibilities. Where should we put the emphasis, on our responsibilities or on our rights?

Take a Christian marriage, for example. It's true that the Bible tells wives to submit to their husbands, and a husband might claim that as his right. But he is also given a corresponding responsibility: to love his wife as Christ loved the Church (and just think what that means). Which should he emphasize: his right or his responsibility?

A wife may nag her husband, because she thinks she has a right to expect him to be the spiritual head of the household. It's true that he has been given that calling by God. She on the other hand has been given a responsibility to love and respect her husband. Where should she put the emphasis, on her right or on her responsibility?

What about parents? Should they focus on their right to expect their children to be obedient? Or on their responsibility, to bring them up in the training and instruction of the Lord, and discipline them when they are disobedient?

Does being a member of a local church give you the right to criticize others or to tear apart someone's doctrine? Or does it give you a responsibility to submit to those in authority over you and relate to others with the same love and acceptance Jesus has shown you?

When we stand before Jesus at the end of our earthly lives, where will He put the emphasis? Will He say to you, "Did those other guys give you everything they should have?" Or will He focus on how well I loved those He put in my care?

If we can learn to serve and love other people without expecting anything in return, it's liberating. Instead of being constantly disappointed by others, we will be truly and pleasantly surprised when people serve and love us.

What About When Others Do Wrong?

What about when other people go wrong? Do we just ignore it?

It's true that we can often see the issues in someone else's life much more clearly than they can but it can take a real struggle for people to acknowledge their failings. Biblically, it is the responsibility of the Holy Spirit to persuade someone of their sin (see John 16:8). You can be sure that He is already gently convicting them. They're already engaged in an internal battle with Him. But the moment we try to intervene and point out the sin, they start to have that struggle with us instead of Him.

PAUSE FOR THOUGHT 2

Spend some time discussing the difference between our rights and responsibilities in relation to others. You may like to consider this in relation to specific people in your life, for example, spouse, child, parent, work colleague, church leader, or neighbor.

"If we can learn to serve and love other people without expecting anything in return, it's liberating. Instead of being constantly disappointed by others, we will be truly and pleasantly surprised when people serve and love us." Do you agree with this? Why/why not?

What would it mean practically for you to focus on your own character and on the needs of others?

Discipline Yes, Judgment No

Jesus was clear that we shouldn't judge others (Matthew 7:1) yet Paul talks about disciplining Christians who do wrong, for example:

> Brothers and sisters, if someone is caught in a sin, you who live by the Spirit should restore that person gently. (Galatians 6:1a)

Judgment and discipline are different things. Judgment is always related to **character**. However, discipline is always related to **behavior**.

Discipline has to be based on something we have seen or heard. If we personally observe another Christian sinning, the Bible tells us to confront the person alone — the objective is to win them back to God.

If they don't repent, then we are to take two or three other witnesses who observed the same sin. If they still won't listen, then we are to tell the church (Matthew 18:15–17). The purpose of this process is not to condemn them, but to restore them to Jesus.

If there are no other witnesses, however, it's just your word against theirs. So the best thing to do is to leave it right there. God knows all about it and He will deal with it in His perfect wisdom. It is His job to bring conviction, not ours.

We are so often tempted to judge a person's character. Suppose I catch a fellow Christian telling an obvious lie, and I confront them. I could say, "You're a liar!" but that would be judgment because I have questioned their character. It would be much better to say, "Did you just say something that's not true?" That calls attention to their **behavior** not their **character**. Better still might be, "You're not a liar. So why did you just say something that's not true?" The truth is, they are a child of God who just acted out of character. The first expression implies that they have the character of a liar and indicates that they cannot change. The other two say nothing about their character. They simply call out a behavior issue. If you point out someone's sinful behavior, you are giving them something they can work with. But calling somebody "a liar," "stupid," "clumsy," "proud," or "evil" is an attack on their character and no one can instantly change their character.

Discipline And Punishment Are Not The Same

Punishment is related to the Old Testament concept of paying evil for evil, "an eye for an eye." It looks backward to the past. God does not punish Christians. The punishment we all deserve fell on Christ.

Discipline, however, looks forward to the future. God may discipline us to in order to develop our character and so that we don't continue to make the same mistakes.

Hebrews 12:5–11 tells us that God's discipline is a proof of His love:

> No discipline seems pleasant at the time, but painful. Later on, however, it produces a harvest of righteousness and peace for those who have been trained by it. (Hebrews 12:11)

So the point of discipline is to help produce a harvest of righteousness and peace, to become more like Jesus.

We have a God who loves us so much, that He sometimes makes the hard choice of allowing us to go through tough circumstances in order to prepare us for the future and to help us become more and more like Jesus in character.

When We Are Attacked

How do we respond if someone attacks us? Look how Jesus reacted when people attacked Him:

> When they hurled their insults at him, he did not retaliate; when he suffered, he made no threats. Instead, he entrusted himself to him who judges justly. (1 Peter 2:23)

We have to learn to do the same. We don't need to defend ourselves any more. If you are wrong, you don't have a defense. If you are right, you don't need a defense. Christ is our defense. We need to entrust ourselves to God and leave the outcome with Him.

If you can learn not to be defensive when someone exposes your character flaws or attacks your performance, you may have an opportunity to turn the situation around and minister to that person.

Nobody tears down another person from a position of strength. Those who are critical of others are either hurting or immature. If we're secure in our own identity in Christ, we can learn not to be defensive when people attack us.

People are unreasonable, illogical, and self-centered.

Love them anyway.

If you do good, people will accuse you of selfish, ulterior motives.

Do good anyway.

If you are successful, you will win false friends and true enemies.

Succeed anyway.

The good you do today will be forgotten tomorrow.

Do good anyway.

Honesty and frankness make you vulnerable.

Be honest and frank anyway.

The biggest people with the biggest ideas can be shot down by the smallest people with the smallest minds.

Think big anyway.

People favor underdogs but follow only top dogs.

Fight for the underdog anyway.

What you spend years building may be destroyed overnight.

Build anyway.

People really need help, but may attack you if you help them.

Help people anyway.

Give the world the best you've got and you'll get kicked in the teeth.

Give the world the best you've got anyway.

Paul says: "If it is possible, as far as it depends on you, live at peace with everyone" (Romans 12:18). The crucial phrase is, "as far as it depends on you." Conflict is a normal part of life. It's nothing to be feared.

You won't always have happy, harmonious relationships with others. It's how you handle it that matters.

On page 184 there is a questionnaire entitled "What Do I Believe?" It will be very helpful if you can complete it before next time.

REFLECTION

Spend some time asking God for wisdom as to how best to relate to others in your life. First, consider who the main people in your life are. Then ask God for wisdom in how you can best relate to them. Is there a need to stop judging their character and instead offer loving discipline? Or to forgive them? How can you meet their needs?

WITNESS

How can you be a good neighbor to those who live on your street? How could you get to know them better, so that you would have a better idea of what their needs are?

IN THE COMING WEEK

Take some time to evaluate your faith by completing the "What Do I Believe?" questionnaire on the following page.

Give some serious thought as to how you would complete the sentences.

What Do I Believe?

	Low				High
1. How successful am I?	1	2	3	4	5

1. How successful am I?   1   2   3   4   5

   I would be more successful if _____

2. How significant am I?   1   2   3   4   5

   I would be more significant if _____

3. How fulfilled am I?   1   2   3   4   5

   I would be more fulfilled if _____

4. How satisfied am I?   1   2   3   4   5

   I would be more satisfied if _____

5. How happy am I?   1   2   3   4   5

   I would be happier if _____

6. How much fun am I having?   1   2   3   4   5

   I would have more fun if _____

7. How secure am I?   1   2   3   4   5

   I would be more secure if _____

8. How peaceful am I?   1   2   3   4   5

   I would have more peace if _____

What Next?

WHAT'S IT ABOUT?

OBJECTIVE: To evaluate what we believe in the light of God's Word and make adjustments where necessary so that we can stay on the path of becoming more like Jesus.

FOCUS VERSE: The goal of this command is love, which comes from a pure heart and a good conscience and a sincere faith (1 Timothy 1:5).

FOCUS TRUTH: Nothing and no one can keep us from being the person God created us to be, but if we want to be truly successful, fulfilled, satisfied, and so on, we need to uncover and throw out false beliefs about what those things mean and commit ourselves to believing the truth in the Bible.

> The accompanying material for this session is in the fourth book in the FREEDOM IN CHRIST DISCIPLESHIP SERIES, *The You God Planned*, pages 13–55.

WELCOME

What would you like to do before the end of your life?

WORSHIP

He will be with us always. Hebrews 13:5–6; Psalm 94:14; Matthew 28:20.

Making Freedom A Way Of Life

> "You did not choose me, but I chose you and appointed you so that you might go and produce fruit, fruit that will last." (John 15:16a)

We don't want this to be one of those courses that you enjoy but then as time passes the principles you learned just fade away. Our objective is that these principles become a part of your everyday life so that you will bear fruit that will last. What we've taught is very straightforward. There are three main points:

1. Know Who You Are In Jesus

You are a holy one who can come boldly into God's presence at any time.

2. Resolve Your Personal And Spiritual Issues

We recommend that you use *The Steps To Freedom In Christ* on a regular basis in the same way that you give your car a regular service.

3. Be Transformed By The Renewing Of Your Mind

Stronghold-busting really works. As you keep building your spiritual muscles, remember it will feel like a complete waste of time but you will see progress as long as you keep working.

The Road Ahead

The "What Do I Believe?" survey on page 184 will help you identify what you actually believe right now. Assuming that your basic needs for food, shelter, and safety are met, we're motivated every day by how we can be successful, significant, secure, and so on. How you answered those questions or the way you completed the sentences: "I would be more successful if," "I would be more significant if" reflects what you really believe and we're going to consider each of those eight areas.

Success Comes From Having The Right Goals

We looked at life-goals back in Session 6. Success is all about whether you achieve your goals. So if you want to be successful in God's terms it's important to understand what His life-goal is for you.

If God wants something done, can it be done? To put it another way, would God ever say, "I have something for you to do. I know you won't be able to do it, but just give it your best shot." That wouldn't be fair! Whatever life-goal God has for you, you can be sure that no circumstance and no person can stop you from achieving it. God loves you too much to give you something you couldn't do.

2 Peter 1:3–8 helps us understand God's life-goal for each one of us.

Peter starts by telling us (in verse 3) that we already have "everything we need for life and godliness." Then he reminds us that we share in God's nature — we are holy through and through. That's a great starting point!

He goes on to show us God's goal for our lives:

> For this very reason, make every effort to add to your faith goodness; and to goodness, knowledge; and to knowledge, self-control; and to self-control, perseverance; and to perseverance, godliness; and to godliness, brotherly kindness; and to brotherly kindness, love. For if you possess these qualities in increasing measure, they will keep you from being ineffective and unproductive in your knowledge of our Lord Jesus Christ. (2 Peter 1:5–10)

We are to start with faith. Then we are to make every effort to build on our faith and add to it these characteristics: goodness, knowledge, self-control, perseverance, godliness, brotherly kindness, and love.

These are all **character** qualities. God's goal for our lives is about building our character. His primary concern is not so much what we **do** but what we are **like**. Because what we **do** flows from who we **are**.

The only person who has ever perfectly reflected the character qualities in that list is Jesus.

The life-goal that God has for you could be defined like this: **To become more and more like Jesus in character.**

The great news is that nobody and nothing on earth can keep you from being the person God planned. Except . . . you!

We saw in Session 6 how negative emotions such as anger, anxiety, and depression can be a warning that you may have some unhealthy life-goals that depend on people or circumstances that you have no right or ability to control.

Think about the pastor whose life-goal was to reach the community for Christ, which is something that could be blocked by every person in the community. A good goal for them might be: "to become the best pastor I can be." As they adopt that goal, they will get rid of a lot of anger, anxiety, and depression and become more and more like Jesus in character. People will follow them and trust them more. Paradoxically they may end up reaching the community for Christ.

Remember the parent whose life-goal was to have a happy, harmonious Christian family. What if they made their goal, "to be the husband and dad or wife and mom that God wants me to be"? Wouldn't that greatly increase the chances of their having a happy, harmonious family?

You may think you don't have enough talents or intelligence to be the person God wants you to be or that the circumstances you find yourself in prevent you from being the person God wants you to be. But there is no mention in Peter's list of talents, intelligence, or positive circumstances. We are not given the same amount of talents: some have one talent, others have ten. We don't all have the same intelligence and our circumstances can be totally different. You might be thinking, "That's not fair!" But God is not measuring you by those things! He's looking at your **character**, not your talent or your intelligence. It's equally possible for a Christian with one talent and a Christian with a ten talents to see their character grow to reach the life-goal God has for each one of us.

PAUSE FOR THOUGHT 1

Look at the questionnaire "What Do I Believe?" on page 184. If you feel comfortable, share with the group where you put your lowest score and what you wrote for that question.

2 Peter 1:3 states that we have "everything we need for life and godliness." Discuss the idea that, whatever life-goal God has for you, no circumstance or person can prevent you from achieving it — except you.

"There is no mention in Peter's list of talents, intelligence, or positive circumstances." How does that change your thinking?

Significance Comes From Proper Use Of Time

What's forgotten in time is of little significance. What's remembered for eternity is of great significance. Significance is about time.

> But Zion said, "The LORD has forsaken me, the Lord has forgotten me."

> "Can a mother forget the baby at her breast and have no compassion on the child she has borne? Though she may forget, I will not forget you! See, I have engraved you on the palms of my hands; your walls are ever before me." (Isaiah 49:14–16)

God uses a graphic illustration — engraving His people on the palm of His hands. God has placed us somewhere where no matter how much time passes, we will not be forgotten. That's how significant we are!

If you want to increase the significance of what you do, focus your time on things that will make an eternal difference.

Fulfillment Comes From Serving Others

Jesus must have been the most fulfilled person that ever walked the earth. Where did He get His sense of fulfillment from? He said, "My food is to do the will of him who sent me and to finish his work" (John 4:34).

> Each one should use whatever gift he has received to serve others, as faithful stewards of God's grace in its various forms. (1 Peter 4:10)

God has made each of us unique. And each one of us has different gifts. Yet we are to use them to serve others — and when we do, paradoxically we become fulfilled.

Fulfillment comes when we "grow where we're planted" instead of looking for better soil or a prettier pot by changing the circumstances or people in our lives.

It's not by accident at all that God has sovereignly placed you in your family, on your street, with your friends, at your job, or at your college.

God has specially planted you to serve Him by serving your family. That's your first and foremost calling. You have a unique role as an ambassador for Christ where you live and where you work. These are your mission fields and you are the worker God has appointed for the harvest there.

God wants Christians who are becoming more and more like Jesus in every area of society. Your calling to business or industry or education or art or the health services, whatever it is, is a high and holy calling where you can make an eternal difference.

Don't try to be someone else. Be the unique person that God has made you to be.

God won't ask me why I wasn't Billy Graham or Mother Theresa. But He might ask me why I wasn't me!

Satisfaction Comes From Living A Quality Life

"Blessed are those who hunger and thirst for righteousness, for they will be filled" (Matthew 5:6).

The truth is that nothing else really satisfies except living a righteous life. If you wrote something like, "I would be more satisfied if I worked harder for righteousness in my community" you are on the right path.

Think about something you purchased that left you dissatisfied. What was the issue? It generally has to do with quality. Satisfaction is an issue of quality. We achieve greater satisfaction from doing a few things well than from doing many things in a haphazard or hasty way. The key to personal satisfaction is not found in doing more things but in deepening commitment to quality in the things that we are already doing.

The same is true in relationships. If you are dissatisfied in your relationships, perhaps you have spread yourself too thin. We can learn from Jesus, who taught thousands and equipped 70 for ministry, but invested most of His time in twelve disciples. Out of those twelve, He selected three — Peter, James, and John — to be with Him at crucial times: on the Mount of Transfiguration, on the Mount of Olives, and in the Garden of Gethsemane. We all need the satisfaction that quality relationships bring.

Happiness Comes From Wanting What We Have

The world's concept of happiness is having what we want. However, never has there been a society where people have so many things yet are so unhappy.

> Godliness with contentment is great gain. For we brought nothing into the world, and we can take nothing out of it. But if we have food and clothing, we will be content with that. (1 Timothy 6:6–8)

Happiness isn't about having what you want. It's about wanting what you have. As long as you're focusing on what you don't have, or what you can't do, you'll be unhappy. But when you begin to appreciate what you already have, you'll be happy all your life.

PAUSE FOR THOUGHT 2

In what ways can we know significance by focusing our time on things that will make an eternal difference?

What causes us to want to be "someone else," rather than growing as the unique person God has made us to be?

Christians can often feel overwhelmed by the many things that demand their time. Discuss the idea that greater satisfaction comes from doing a few things well, rather than from doing many things in a haphazard or hasty way.

Fun Comes From Enjoying Life Moment-By-Moment

You may think fun is a strange thing to include in this list. Yet of all people, a Christian who has been set free by Christ, and knows who they are and what they have in Him, should be having fun!

Often when you plan for fun, it leads to a let-down because it doesn't turn out as expected. Most fun happens spontaneously when we throw off our inhibitions, when we stop worrying what other people will think of us.

> If I were still trying to please men, I would not be a servant of Christ. (Galatians 1:10)

Do you still find yourself thinking, "What will people say?" Those walking in freedom will respond, "Who cares what people say? I'm not playing to the crowd any longer. I'm playing for God alone."

When David got the ark of the covenant back, he was so happy that he leapt and danced before the Lord in celebration. His wife, Michal, was embarrassed by his behavior and told him so in no uncertain terms. David said, "I will celebrate before the LORD. I will become even more undignified than this" (2 Samuel 6:21b–22a). The embarrassment that can prevent us from having fun may also hold us back from telling others about Jesus if we do not make a constant effort to throw it off.

Our wonderful, loving, creative God is not a killjoy. When we are free, we can laugh. We don't need to keep up appearances.

Security Comes From Focusing On Eternal Values

Jesus said that no one can snatch us out of His hand (John 10:27–29). Paul declared that nothing can separate us from the love of God in Christ (Romans 8:35–39). You cannot get more secure than that!

We can, however, feel insecure when we depend upon earthly things that we have no right or ability to control.

Every "thing" we now have we shall some day lose.

> "He is no fool to give up that which he cannot keep in order to gain that which he cannot lose."
>
> Jim Eliot (a missionary who was murdered)

Peace Comes From Quieting The Inner Storm

Jesus is the Prince of Peace (Isaiah 9:6) and He said:

> My peace I give you. I do not give as the world gives. Do not let your hearts be troubled and do not be afraid. (John 14:27)

The peace of God is something we need to take hold of every day in our inner person. A lot of things may disrupt our external world because we can't control all of our circumstances and relationships. But we can control the inner world of our thoughts and emotions by allowing the peace of God to rule in our hearts on a daily basis.

There may be chaos all around us, but God is bigger than any storm.

Nothing will happen to you today that God and you cannot handle.

Difficulties Help Us Toward The Goal

You may think that your past or present circumstances are so difficult that they stop you from becoming the person God wants you to be but actually the opposite is true. Paul says that we can rejoice in our sufferings because "we know that suffering produces perseverance; perseverance, character; and character, hope" (Romans 5:3–4).

> Consider it pure joy, my brothers and sisters, whenever you face trials of many kinds, because you know that the testing of your faith produces perseverance. Let perseverance finish its work so that you may be mature and complete, not lacking anything. (James 1:2–4)

Persevering through difficulties develops our character and helps us fulfill our life-goal to become more and more like Jesus.

Defeated spouses say, "My marriage is hopeless," then try to solve the problem by changing partners. Others feel their jobs or churches are hopeless. So they move, only to discover that their new job or church is just as hopeless. Those difficult situations may be helping you achieve God's goals for your life. There are legitimate times to change jobs or churches, but if we are just running from our own immaturity, it will follow us wherever we go.

We need occasional mountain-top experiences, but the fertile soil for growth is always down in the valleys, not on the mountain tops.

It's The First Day Of The Rest Of Your Life

We're all going to die. One day you will lose everything you have, including your closest relationships, your qualifications, your possessions, and your money.

The only thing that you will not lose is your relationship with Jesus and everything that comes with it.

That is why Paul can say, "For to me, to live is Christ and to die is gain" (Philippians 1:21).

If you try putting anything else other than Christ in that verse, it doesn't work:

For me to live is my career, to die is . . . loss.

For me to live is my family, to die is . . . loss.

For me to live is a successful Christian ministry, to die is . . . loss.

But when the point of our life here and now is simply Jesus and becoming like Him, when we die it just gets better.

Whether or not you feel you are very far along the path of becoming more like Jesus, you can leave here in the sure knowledge that you are God's holy child and that He delights in you. He is intimately concerned in your life and has plans to give you a hope and a future (Jeremiah 29:11).

Are you ready to adopt God's goal for your life, to become more and more like Jesus in character?

This was written by someone (of unknown source) who decided to take God at His word:

> I am part of the "Fellowship of the unashamed." I have Holy Spirit Power. The die has been cast. I've stepped over the line. The decision has been made. I am a disciple of His. I won't look back, let up, slow down, back away, or be still. My past is redeemed, my present makes sense, and my future is secure. I am finished and done with low-living, sight-walking, small-planning, smooth knees, colorless dreams, tame visions, mundane talking, miserly giving, and dwarfed goals!
>
> I no longer need pre-eminence, prosperity, position, promotions, plaudits, or popularity. I don't have to be right, first, top, recognized, praised, regarded or rewarded. I now live by presence, lean by faith, love by patience, lift by prayer and labor by power.
>
> My face is set, my gait is fast, my goal is heaven, my road is narrow, my way is rough, my companions few, my guide reliable, my mission clear. I cannot be bought, compromised, detoured, lured away, turned back, diluted, or delayed. I will not flinch in the face of sacrifice, hesitate in the presence of adversity, negotiate at the table of the enemy, ponder at the pool of popularity, or meander in the maze of mediocrity.
>
> I won't give up, shut up, let up, or burn up till I've preached up, prayed up, paid up, stored up and stayed up for the cause of Christ.
>
> I am a disciple of Jesus. I must go till He comes, give till I drop, preach till all know, and work till He stops.
>
> And when He comes to get His own, He'll have no problems recognizing me. My colors will be clear.

The rest of your life is ahead of you. You can become the person God wants you to be. Nothing and no one can get in your way!

REFLECTION

Discuss the idea that God's goal for your life is that you become more and more like Jesus in character. What would it look like for you to embrace that?

Spend some time in prayer committing to God's goal for your life and thanking Him that you can achieve it in His strength.

Spend some time thanking God for what He has shown and taught you through the course. Ask God what steps He wants you to take next.

 WITNESS

Pick two or three of the eight areas we have considered. How would not-yet-Christians around you be affected if you were to put the principles into practice?

 IN THE COMING WEEK

Work out which of the eight areas in the "What Do I Believe?" questionnaire are the most challenging for you. Spend some time reading the relevant passages for those areas in "God's Guidelines for the Walk of Faith" on page 200 of your Participant's Guide. You could use them to develop a stronghold-buster for the ongoing renewing of your mind.

God's Guidelines For The Walk Of Faith

Success comes from having the right goals

Success is accepting God's goal for our lives and by His grace becoming what He has called us to be (Joshua 1:7, 8; 2 Peter 1:3–10; 3 John 2).

Significance comes from proper use of time

What is forgotten in time is of little significance. What is remembered for eternity is of greatest significance (1 Corinthians 3:13; Acts 5:33–40; 1 Timothy 4:7, 8).

Fulfilment comes from serving others

Fulfilment is discovering our own uniqueness in Christ and using our gifts to build others up and glorify the Lord (2 Timothy 4:5; Romans 12:1–18; Matthew 25:14–30).

Satisfaction comes from living a quality life

Satisfaction is living righteously and seeking to raise the quality of our relationships and the things we do (Matthew 5:5; Proverbs 18:24; 2 Timothy 4:7).

Happiness comes from wanting what we have

Happiness is being thankful for what we do have, rather than focusing on what we don't have — because happy are the people who want what they have (Philippians 4:12; 1 Thessalonians 5:18; 1 Timothy 6:6–8)!

Fun comes from enjoying life moment by moment

The secret is to remove unbiblical hindrances such as keeping up appearances (2 Samuel 6:20–23; Galatians 1:10, 5:1; Romans 14:22).

Security comes from focusing on eternal values

Insecurity comes when we depend on things that will pass away rather than things that will last for ever (John 10:27–30; Romans 8:31–39; Ephesians 1:13, 14).

Peace comes from quieting the inner storm

The peace of God is internal, not external (Jeremiah 6:14; John 14:27; Philippians 4:6, 7; Isaiah 32:17).

Faulty Thinking (Lies)

What God Says (Truth)

Faulty Thinking (Lies)	What God Says (Truth)

Faulty Thinking (Lies)	What God Says (Truth)

Faulty Thinking (Lies)	What God Says (Truth)

Song Lyrics

WORSHIP
IN SPIRIT & TRUTH

16 songs inspired by the message of Freedom In Christ
featuring Testricity, Nicole C. Mullen, The Katinas and others

Songs To Take The Truths Deeper

Worship In Spirit And Truth is an album of 16 powerful new songs inspired by the *Freedom In Christ Course*. These brand new songs reflect the truths taught and will help you take them from head to heart.

The album was produced in Nashville by Testricity Music Group and features Testricity, Nicole C. Mullen, The Katinas, and other artists.

Wayne and Esther Tester formed the band Testricity and the record label Testricity Music Group out of their desire to see people set free in Christ. They have written and produced over 500 songs for Universal, Garth Brooks, Disney, Dreamworks, LifeWay, and others. Wayne wrote the theme song for the Sydney Olympics which was seen by 3.6 billion people at one time and has won many awards, (Dove, Platinum records, ASCAP, etc.). But when he went through the *Freedom In Christ Course*, he realized he had issues with pride and performance and had made God's gifts an idol. So he put all of his awards in the trash and put on his eternal true identity in Jesus Christ. The truths in the *Freedom In Christ Course* helped Esther take hold of her freedom from an abusive past. You can see them tell their story on the Freedom In Christ app.

Nicole C. Mullen is a singer-songwriter who has been inducted into the Christian Music Hall of Fame. She is the only African-American artist to win a Dove Award for both Song of the Year and Songwriter of the Year. On the app she shares the story of how her son was hugely helped by Freedom In Christ's teaching.

The songs are available for purchase on CD or download. They are also available as lyric videos to make them easy to use in worship.

The song lyrics are printed on the following pages.

For further information and to download go to: FICMinternational.org/songs

Come Closer

After a middle-of-the-night battle with major spiritual warfare, I started saying over and over and then singing in desperation these words, "Come closer, I need You to come closer." I kept on praying and singing this for about an hour and then sat down at the piano and within 30 minutes, the song was finished. God used this song to begin my freedom journey. — Wayne Tester

Beautiful, so beautiful
Your love is working deep in me
Adonai, sweet Adonai
Your love is rising up in me

Come closer
I need You to come closer
I open up my heart
I open up my heart
Come closer
I need You to come closer
I want to know Your heart
I want to know Your heart
Jesus
I love Your Name, Jesus

El Shaddai, my El Shaddai
I long for You, my heart's desire
Emmanuel, Emmanuel
My God with me, my Holy Fire

(Repeat Chorus)

You know Your plans for me
Open my eyes to see
Lord, give me victory
Abundant grace
My heart cries out to You
Your living Word I trust
I need Your healing touch
I seek Your face
Come closer

(Repeat Chorus)

Words & Music by Wayne Tester.
© 2017 Tester Electricity Music (ASCAP) (admin. by Music Services).
℗ & © 2017 Testricity Music Group. ALL RIGHTS RESERVED.

That's Who I Am (Part One of Four)

After Esther and I went through the FIC Course I woke up in the middle of the night and God shared with me that I needed to keep myself away from idols. I went into my studio, gathered up all my music awards, and threw them in the trash. I had struggled for years with believing the lie that I had to perform to gain approval. Esther and I both had the same idea about putting the "Who Am I?" list to music. The song has made a huge impact on us. We are now singing God's truths at all hours of the day and night and it's a constant source of inspiration. — Wayne Tester

I am the salt of the earth
(echo)
I am the light of the world
(echo)
I am a child of God (echo)

I am part of the true vine
(echo)
A channel of Christ's life
(echo)
I am Christ's friend (echo)

I am chosen and appointed
(echo)
By Christ to bear His fruit
(echo)
I am a slave of righteousness
(echo)
I am enslaved to God (echo)

I am a son of God (echo)
God is spiritually my Father
(echo)
I am a joint heir with Christ
(echo)
Sharing His inheritance with
Him (echo)

I am a temple (echo)
A dwelling place of God
(echo)
His Spirit and His life (echo)
Dwell in me (echo)

(All sing)
I am not the great "I am"
But by the grace of God, I am
what I am
I am not the great "I am"
But by the grace of God, I am
what I am
I am not the great "I am"
But by the grace of God, I am
what I am
I am not the great "I am"
But by the grace of God, I am
what I am

That's who I am (echo)
That's who I am (echo)
That's who I am (echo)
That's who I am (echo)

Words by Neil T. Anderson, Wayne Tester, Esther Tester.
Music by Wayne Tester, Esther Tester.

Eyes Of Faith

During a particular "perfect storm" of circumstances in life, the old hymn *Be Thou My Vision* popped into my head as I struggled with pride, panic attacks, and anxiety. I loved the idea of combining something old with something new and the rest is history with this song. I pray it will be as much of an encouragement to others as it has for me. — Wayne Tester

You are my vision, oh Lord of
my heart
Nothing compares to You,
bright Morning Star
You're my best thought, by
day and by night
Waking or sleeping, Your
presence my light

You give me eyes of faith
You are my only Truth
You shine Your light so I see
You
You are my guiding lamp
A lighthouse in the night
My vision now and for always
You give me eyes of faith

You are my wisdom, You are
my true Word
I ever with You and You with
me, Lord
You're my great Father, and
I'm Your true son
You in me dwelling, and I with
You one

(Repeat chorus)

I choose to believe in Your
Truth
I choose to keep my eyes on
You

(Repeat Chorus)

That's Who I Am (Part Two of Four)

I grew up with all brothers and I both enjoyed and hated being the only girl. I loved being "daddy's little princess" but it seemed that I didn't get to participate in some of the activities my brothers did and in my teens I was more restricted in where I could go by myself. However, I'm not promised any less of an inheritance in Christ just because I'm a woman and I know full well that I'm every bit as dangerous to the devil as my spiritual brothers are. In Christ, I am like a SON and I LOVE that!
— Esther Tester

I am united to the Lord (echo)
And am one spirit with Him (echo)
I am a member of Christ's body (echo)

I am a new creation (echo)
I am reconciled to God (echo)
And am a minister of reconciliation (echo)

I am a son of God (echo)
And one in Christ (echo)
I am an heir of God (echo)
Since I am a son of God (echo)

I am a saint (echo)
I am God's workmanship (echo)
His handiwork (echo)
Born anew in Christ to do His work (echo)

I am a fellow citizen (echo)
With the rest of God's family (echo)

I am a prisoner of Christ (echo)
I am righteous and holy (echo)

(All sing)
I am not the great "I am"
But by the grace of God, I am what I am
I am not the great "I am"
But by the grace of God, I am what I am
I am not the great "I am"
But by the grace of God, I am what I am
I am not the great "I am"
But by the grace of God, I am what I am

That's who I am (echo)
That's who I am (echo)
That's who I am (echo)
That's who I am (echo)

Words by Neil T. Anderson, Wayne Tester, Esther Tester.
Music by Wayne Tester, Esther Tester.
© 2017 Tester Electricity Music (ASCAP) / Fuzzy Socks Music (BMI) (both admin. by Music Services).
℗ & © 2017 Testricity Music Group. ALL RIGHTS RESERVED.

We Choose Life

Words have a powerful effect on us, either for good or for bad. We've lived with believing this world's lies far too long. We wanted to put a stake in the ground and say, "We choose life instead of death." We wanted this song to be a unified declaration between us all to sing together, "We Choose Life." — Wayne and Esther Tester

You are near us now
We will follow You
You give life and love
All Your ways are true
We will walk with You
And keep Your commands
So that You may bless
With Your faithful hands

We choose life, we choose life
We love You Lord our God
And place our faith in You
We turn away from sin to
know what is true
We choose life, we choose life

May we grow in love
And know more of You
You're our help and guide
You're the Way and Truth
As we turn to You
As we listen now
May Your holy Word
In our hearts resound

(Repeat Chorus)

Your holy Word renews our minds
Transformed, we are made new in Christ
We walk by faith and not by sight
And by Your Spirit, not by our might

(Repeat Chorus)

Words & Music by Wayne Tester, Esther Tester.
© 2017 Tester Electricity Music (ASCAP) / Fuzzy Socks Music (BMI) (both admin. by Music Services).
℗ & © 2017 Testricity Music Group. ALL RIGHTS RESERVED.

That's Who I Am (Part Three of Four)

Even though my flesh is still a work in progress, my spirit is just as perfect as it became when I first knew Jesus when I was seven years old. I love to close my eyes and see myself seated in Heaven because that's actually where I am . . . right now. When David wrote my favorite psalm, Psalm 84, he was talking about where he actually was, in the dwelling place of God, not some place he wished he was. We are not guests in His house, we live there, right now. Let that just blow your mind for a minute. — Esther Tester

I am a citizen of heaven
(echo)
Seated in heaven right now
(echo)
I am hidden with Christ in
God (echo)

I'm an expression of the life
of Christ (echo)
Because He is my life (echo)
I am chosen of God, holy and
dearly loved (echo)

I am a son of light (echo)
And not of darkness (echo)
I am a holy partaker (echo)
Of a heavenly calling (echo)

I'm a partaker of Christ
(echo)
I share in His life (echo)
I am one of God's living
stones (echo)
Being built up in Christ as a
spiritual house (echo)

I am a member (echo)
Of a chosen race (echo)
A royal priesthood (echo)
A holy nation (echo)
A people for God's own
possession (echo)

(All sing)
I am not the great "I am"
But by the grace of God, I am
what I am
I am not the great "I am"
But by the grace of God, I am
what I am
I am not the great "I am"
But by the grace of God, I am
what I am
I am not the great "I am"
But by the grace of God, I am
what I am

That's who I am (echo)
That's who I am (echo)
That's who I am (echo)
That's who I am (echo)

Words by Neil T. Anderson, Wayne Tester, Esther Tester.
Music by Wayne Tester, Esther Tester.
© 2017 Tester Electricity Music (ASCAP) / Fuzzy Socks Music (BMI)
(both admin. by Music Services).
℗ & © 2017 Testricity Music Group. ALL RIGHTS RESERVED.

Living In Colour

I was unhappy and couldn't figure out why. So I went on vacation thinking that would replenish my smile . . . but it didn't. So, walking along Florida's beach voted "most beautiful in the nation" yet feeling completely miserable, I read Proverbs 27:20 and I realized that as long as my desires didn't line up with God's, I would never be happy. I changed that day. Everything changed that day. — Esther Tester

Desire is like the grave
It can't be satisfied
Soulsick to pierce the gray
Searching for truth in lies

My spirit cries out loud
And defies my fear and doubt

Praise the Lord, oh my soul
All my inmost being, praise
Your Holy Name
Praise the Lord, oh my soul
Every part of me is now a
different shade
Living in colour
Now I'm living in colour

Arise, o' dawn of day
With my new song of light
Above the clouds of gray
The sun defies the night

I'm waking from the lies
Truth has opened up my eyes

(Repeat Chorus)

I will live, I will live by the
Spirit of God
I am His, I am His, purchased
by His blood
I believe, I believe I'm on
eagle's wings
I receive, I receive, I am free
to sing
(repeat)

(Repeat Chorus)

Words & Music by Wayne Tester, Esther Tester.
© 2017 Tester Electricity Music (ASCAP) / Fuzzy Socks Music (BMI)
(both admin. by Music Services).
℗ & © 2017 Testricity Music Group. ALL RIGHTS RESERVED.

That's Who I Am (Part Four of Four)

Wayne and I are sci-fi junkies. We actually have enough Star Trek ornaments to cover an entire Christmas tree. So the fact that the Bible tells us we are "aliens" or strangers in this world really strikes a fun chord with us. But on a serious note, it helps us to put things in perspective. This world and everything in it will come to an end. I don't belong to this world. I am a citizen of Heaven! — Esther Tester

I am an alien (echo)
And stranger to this world (echo)
In which I temporarily live (echo)

I am an enemy of the devil (echo)
I am a child of God (echo)
And I will resemble Christ when He returns (echo)

I am born of God (echo)
And the evil one cannot touch me (echo)
No, the devil cannot touch me (echo)

(All sing)
I am not the great "I am"
But by the grace of God, I am what I am
I am not the great "I am"
But by the grace of God, I am what I am
I am not the great "I am"
But by the grace of God, I am what I am
I am not the great "I am"
But by the grace of God, I am what I am

That's who I am (echo)
That's who I am (echo)
That's who I am (echo)
That's who I am (echo)

Words by Neil T. Anderson, Wayne Tester, Esther Tester.
Music by Wayne Tester, Esther Tester.
© 2017 Tester Electricity Music (ASCAP) / Fuzzy Socks Music (BMI) (both admin. by Music Services).
℗ & © 2017 Testricity Music Group. ALL RIGHTS RESERVED.

Standing Stronger

We all come to a point in life when we need to put a stake in the ground. This is that song. 'Nuf said. — Wayne and Esther Tester

Your divine power
Has given me all that I need
To live a life of godliness
'Cause I know You, the One
who made me

You called me by Your glory
You called me by Your
goodness
You've given me a story
Makes me wanna sing

I'm standing stronger
Than I could ever stand on
my own
Here in Your power
There's nothing that I can't
overcome
When I'm standing in the
power of Your love

Every hour
You're giving me all that I
need

To live a life of holiness
Oh, I love You, the One who
made me

You called me by Your glory
You called me by Your
goodness
You've given me a story
Makes me wanna sing

(Repeat Chorus)

You called me by Your glory
You called me by Your
goodness
You've given me a story
Makes me wanna sing
(repeat)
Makes me wanna sing

(Repeat Chorus)

When I'm standing in the
power of Your love

Ever Present God (Psalm 139)

I feel a kinship to King David, author of the Psalms, because it was more natural for him to sing about God than to speak about Him. I hope that as you sing this Psalm you will recapture some of the original "heart" of David, the man after God's own heart. — Wayne Tester

Oh Lord, You have searched
me and known me
You know when I lay down
and when I rise up
And from heaven You discover
my thoughts
You observe my wanderings
and my dreaming
You are aware of all my ways

Before a word is on my
tongue, You know all about it,
Lord
You have encircled me; You
have placed Your hand on me
This extraordinary knowledge
is beyond me
It is higher; I am unable to
reach it

Where can I hide to escape
Your Spirit
Where can I flee from Your
presence
If I climb to the sky, You are
there
If I go underground, You are
there
If I live at the eastern horizon
or settle at the western limits
Even there Your hand will
lead me

Your right hand would hold
on to me

If I say, "Let the darkness
hide me
And let the light around me
turn into night"
Even in darkness I cannot
hide from You
To You the night shines bright
as day
Darkness and light are the
same to You

You are the One who created
my deepest parts
You formed me in my
mother's womb
I will praise You, for I am
fearfully and wonderfully
made
Your works are miraculous
And my soul knows it very
well

My bones were not hidden
from You
When I was made in secret
When I was formed in the
depths of the earth

Your eyes saw me when I was
formless
All my days were written in
Your book
And planned before a single
one of them began

How precious also are Your
thoughts
Concerning me, oh God
How vast their sum is
If I counted them, they would
outnumber the grains of sand
When I wake up, I am still
with You

God, do away with
wickedness for good
Keep away from me, those
who thirst for blood
Who speak against You
wickedly

Your enemies take Your name
in vain
Oh Lord, shouldn't I hate
those who hate You
See how I loathe all this
godless arrogance
I hate it with all my heart
Your enemies are my
enemies

Search me, God, and know
my heart
Test me and know my
concerns
See if there is any sinful way
in me
Lead me in the everlasting
way

My Father

Events in my life left me wallowing in self-pity and low self-esteem. "I am the apple of God's eye" was just a phrase and seemed foreign to me. This song was born out of my need to know that I really matter to God. — Wayne Tester

I believe You are intimate
And involved with me
So kind and compassionate
Always with me
Slow to anger
Full of mercy
In You I'm complete

Heavenly Father, You are my Father
I am the apple of Your eye, my Father
Heavenly Father, You are my Father
I am the apple of Your eye, my Father

I believe You are full of joy
And You're proud of me
So warm and affectionate
Holy, complete
Tender hearted and forgiving
You have made me clean

(Repeat Chorus 2x)

Freely Forgive

My greatest healing has come when I have made the choice to forgive. It starts with admitting to myself who I need to forgive. Then, in my mind, I write out a check to that person to pay for the damages that they caused. The real freedom comes when I realize that my bank account is being perpetually replenished with the forgiveness that God has shown me and continues to show to me. Because He forgave me first, I have the capacity and "funds" to forgive others. — Esther Tester

Forgive our sins as we forgive
You taught us, Lord to pray
But You alone can grant us grace
To live the words we say
To live the words we say

How can Your pardon reach and bless
The unforgiving heart
That broods on wrongs and will not let
Old bitterness depart
Old bitterness depart

You freely forgave, so we forgive
We freely forgive our brothers
You freely forgave, so we forgive
We freely forgive our sisters
O-o-oh, o-o-oh

In blazing light Your cross reveals
The truth we dimly knew
What trivial debts are owed to us
How great our debt to You
How great our debt to You

Lord cleanse the depths within our souls
And bound resentment cease
Then bound to all in bonds of love
Our lives will spread Your peace
Our lives will spread Your peace

(Repeat Chorus 2x)

Words by Rosamond E. Herklots. Addt'l words by Wayne Tester, Esther Tester
Music: Scottish Psalter, Wayne Tester, Esther Tester
© Words: 1969 Oxford University Press / © Music: 2017 Tester Electricity Music (ASCAP) / Fuzzy Socks Music (BMI) (admin. by Music Services).
℗ & © 2017 Testricity Music Group. ALL RIGHTS RESERVED.

Butterfly

Change is hard. Really hard if it's real change. Consistently saying "no" to myself and "yes" to God is one of the hardest things for me to do. But it's worth it in the end. After I've pushed through the stubbornness, pride, fear, and pain, I feel like I could fly! It's wonderful when I'm finally free of a behavior that was holding me back! — Esther Tester

Torn, stained and broken
Afraid to be free
I was still a child inside
I was so afraid to fly

Through silent dark
You held my heart
You were calling me "holy"
You were calling me "free"

I am free
The stone is rolled away
I am free
The sun is on my face
I was lost in pride and
blinded by the pain
Then You set me free and
called me from the grave

Fly, fly
Break free from this chrysalis
Fly, butterfly
Spread your wings
Touch the sky
Butterfly, butterfly, butterfly

Truth was a fire
That burned off my fears
Finally I was breaking
through
You were making all things
new

Your love has won
My chains undone
Now I'm standing here holy
Now I'm standing here free

(Repeat Chorus)

Fly, fly
You're free from this
chrysalis
Fly, butterfly
Spread your wings
Touch the sky
Butterfly, butterfly, butterfly

One

We've worshipped along with Nicole C. Mullen at church for years and have always wanted to collaborate on something creative with her but the timing wasn't right. So as we were writing for the FIC Course, it happened. God set up a divine appointment right there in the church aisle and that's when we all knew this was the time. There is disunity wherever you look. There's no better time than now for the church to step up and lead as a unified body. This was the beat that was pulsing in each of our hearts as we wrote this song. If we don't act like the one body we are, then how will they ever see Jesus in us? — Wayne and Esther Tester

You and me may not always
see identically
And there's some things
where we're simply gonna
disagree
A tune of many notes can still
have harmony, a symphony
'Cause I need you and
brother, you need me

And they'll know we are one
By the way we love, by the
way we love
And they'll know we are one
By the way we love, by the
way we love

Take my hand and walk a
mile with me and you will see
Together we can conquer
anything in unity
Through the blood of Christ
He turns diversity to family

'Cause I need you and sister,
you need me

(Repeat Chorus)

There is just one Spirit
One hope, one body
We believe, we believe
There is one baptism
One faith and Lord of all
We believe, we believe

(Repeat Chorus 2x)

By the way we love, by the
way we love
By the way we love, by the
way we love

It's A Brave New World

One of the hardest things we ever have to do is leave the past behind. But we can do it! It takes bravery and trusting that God's going to protect us when we step out onto the water. We're excited for you as you come to the end of this course and go out into that brave new world! — Wayne and Esther Tester

What is forgotten, forgotten
by time doesn't matter
anymore
What is eternal, eternally
mine, will I take to Heaven's
door
All that I'll ever need I have
now in Christ
This is the first day of the rest
of my life

It's a brave new world
I'm leaving my past behind
It's a brave new world
I know who I am in Christ
I believe, I believe
Jesus gave me the victory
I'm renewed, I'm redeemed
It's a brave new world for me
I'm flyin' free
I'm flyin' free

I won't be shaken, I won't be
slowed down 'cause my past
has been redeemed
Looking to Heaven, my future
is now, dreamin' how the
Father dreams
I am transformed by the
renewing of my mind
Each day becoming more and
more like Jesus Christ

(Repeat Chorus 2x)

My New Name

This song was written out of "stuck-ness" in my life. When I started singing these truths that I had read about in Freedom In Christ, I started believing that the past really is in the past and that God is all about making all things new, including me.
— Wayne Tester

Beloved, so beautiful
Protected, unashamed
Forgiven, presentable
In Jesus

My new name
My new name
Thank You, Father God
For my new name

Established, Your work of art
Adopted, I am free
So treasured, I am loved
In Jesus

(Repeat Chorus)

In Christ I am made holy
In Christ complete
In Christ I am made holy
In Christ complete

(Repeat Chorus 2x)

Words & Music by Wayne Tester.
© 2017 Tester Electricity Music (ASCAP) (admin. by Music Services).
℗ & © 2017 Testricity Music Group. ALL RIGHTS RESERVED.

Become A Friend Of FIC

Are you excited about the effect this teaching can have on individuals, churches, and communities? Please help us make the greatest possible impact.

Join our team of international supporters

Freedom In Christ Ministries International exists to equip the Church worldwide to make fruitful disciples. We rely heavily for financial support on people who have understood how important it is to give leaders the tools that will enable them to help people become fruitful disciples, not just converts, especially when we are opening up an office in a new country. Typically your support will be used to:

- help us equip church leaders around the world
- help people overseas establish national Freedom In Christ offices
- translate the FIC Course and our other material into other languages
- partner with other organizations worldwide to equip leaders
- develop further training and equipping resources

Join the team of supporters in your country

We are passionate about working with those who have themselves been touched by the Biblical message of freedom. Financial support enables us to develop new resources and get them into the hands of more church leaders. As a result many, many people are connecting with this life-changing message. There are always new projects — small and large — that don't happen unless there's funding.

To find out more please go to: **FICMinternational.org/friends**